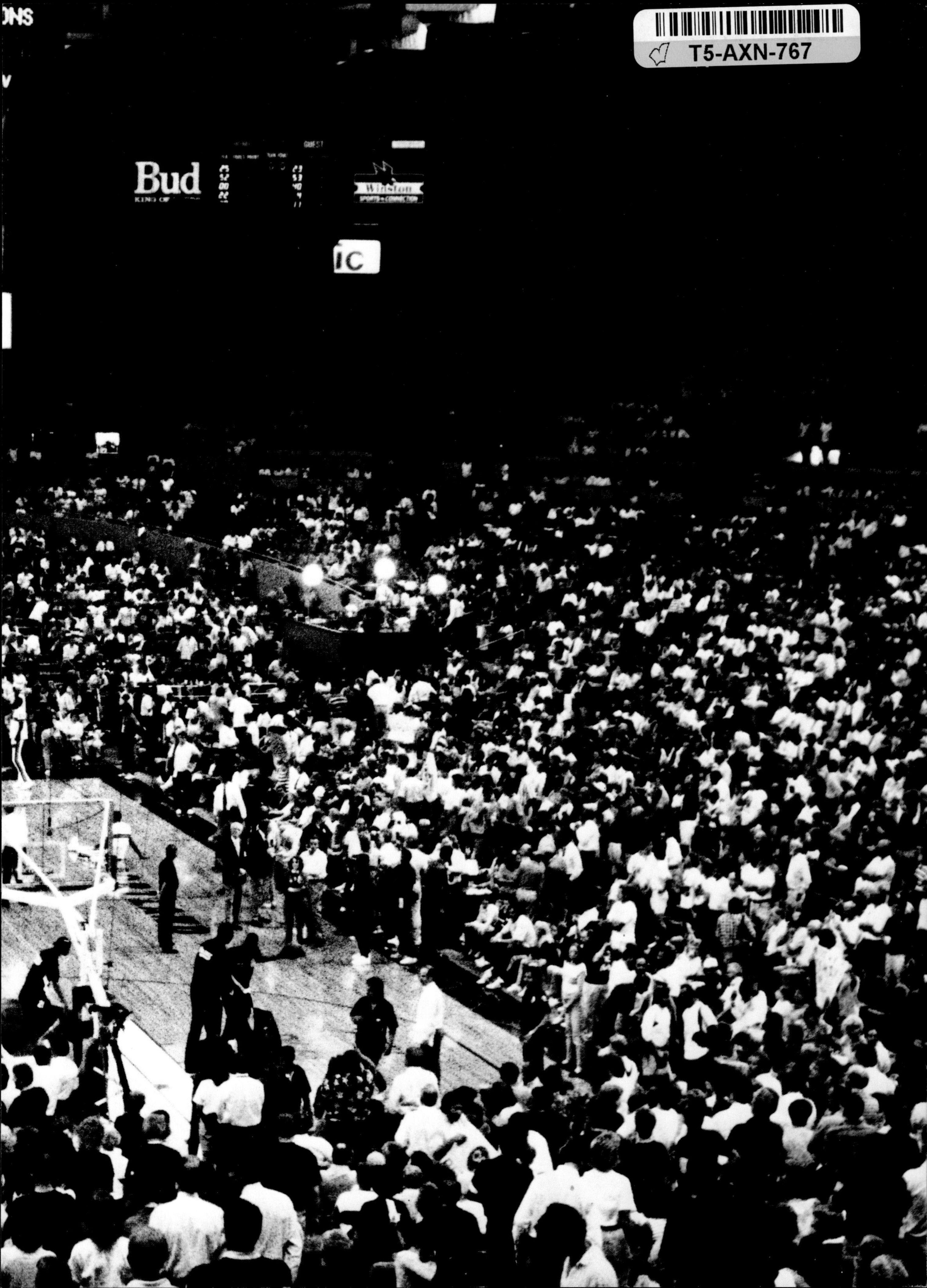
Bud

The Detroit Pistons
1990-91

by Roland Lazenby

Photographs by Kirthmon Dozier
of *The Detroit News*

TAYLOR PUBLISHING COMPANY
Dallas, Texas

Design by Karen Snidow Lazenby

©1990, Roland Lazenby
Taylor Publishing Company
1550 West Mockingbird Lane, Dallas, Texas 75235

Library of Congress Cataloging-in-Publication Data

Lazenby, Roland.
    The Detroit Pistons : 1990-91 / Roland Lazenby.
            p.   cm.
    ISBN 0-87833-755-5
    1. Detroit Pistons (Basketball team)   I. Title
GV885.52.D47L39   1990   89-5051
796.323 '64' 0977434--dc20   CIP

Printed in the United States of America

Contents

The Palace feasts on another foe.

Preface

Welcome to the third edition of the Detroit Pistons yearbook. As with previous editions, it reflects the efforts and involvement of many people.

Many thanks go to the Detroit Pistons' public relations staff—Matt Dobek, Debbie Mayfield and Dave Wieme. Matt compiled the information for Piston Profiles and wrote the bios.

In addition, I want to recognize the editorial assistance of Bob Hartman.

Much credit goes to Arnold Hanson, the publisher at Taylor Publishing Company who first suggested this project and who continues to support it.

I also owe much to the book's primary editor, Jim Donovan at Taylor.

A number of people were gracious in granting interviews, most of which were brief post-game, locker-room sessions. They include Gerald Henderson, Magic Johnson, Jerry West, Elgin Baylor, Bill Laimbeer, Joe Dumars, John Salley, Dennis Rodman, Jack McCloskey, James Edwards, Rick Adelman, Mark Aguirre, Isiah Thomas, and Chuck Daly.

The book would be drab were it not for the outstanding photographic contributions of Kirthmon Dozier. And the staff at Taylor Publishing, led by art director Carol Trammel, has carried the production load with professionalism.

Extensive use was made of a variety of publications, including the *Chicago Tribune, Chicago Sun Times, The Detroit News, The Detroit Free Press, Flint Journal, The Oakland Press, Los Angeles Times, The National, The Oregonian, Sport, Sports Illustrated*, and *The Sporting News*.

The work of a variety of beat writers and columnists has been a vital aid in this project. That group includes the following: Mitch Albom, Bryan Burwell, Shelby Strother, Charlie Vincent, Drew Sharp, Terry Foster, Steve Addy, Dean Howe, Bob Wojnowski, Corky Meinecke, Steve Kornacki, Bill Halls, Joe Falls, Jerry Green, and Michelle Kaufmann.

In addition, a reading of *The Franchise* by Cameron Stauth provided interesting background material.

Roland Lazenby

Delighted to be hot.

Bad Medicine

It was surgery, they cut it so close. But at each critical point in the 1990 Finals, the Detroit Pistons sliced it just the right way. Using their perimeter shooting like scalpels and lasers, they made a nice filet of the Portland Trail Blazers. Laid 'em bare to the gullet, exposing their frailties and weaknesses.

When it was over, the Bad Boys sewed 'em up and left 'em looking like new, except for the very finest of scars on the chest cavity right above the heart. Just like any operation, the patient was a bit groggy afterward and unsure exactly what had happened. There was even a hint of malpractice.

But, naahhh.

It was clean.

In fact, it was pure medical theater. Better even than "St. Elsewhere," this was "The Doctor Always Rings Twice."

Zeke Thomas, M.D., spent most of the 1990 NBA Finals bloody to his elbows, under the bright lights, sweat rolling off his brow, calling for clamps to stop the flow, all the while calmly rearranging the innards of the Western Conference's best team.

When Dr. Zeke wearied, Dr. Vinnie, the cardiologist, stepped in and tidied things up. And they got an assist from Dr. Laimbeer, of the Flop University School of Medicine, who did the anesthesiology. He gassed 'em good.

Their performance was pure brilliance.

Appropriately, they had made medical history, these operators in short pants. More specifically, they had made a modern house call, conducting major surgery right in Portland's very own home, on the table at Memorial Coliseum, before the Blazers' family and friends and a national television audience.

Who'd have thunk the Bad Boys could do it this way? Their reputation had been seeded in thuggery, not precision. Their image was black and

The way they handled the patient would have made Marcus Welby proud. Who said medicine was an art? In June 1990, the Bad Boys made it seem like science.

blue, not teal and white.

But the way they handled the patient would have made Marcus Welby proud. Who said medicine was an art? In June 1990, the Bad Boys made it seem like science.

QUESTIONS, QUESTIONS

While the season ended with precision, it certainly didn't begin that way.

Somewhere along the line, the Pistons had gotten the idea that winning the 1989 NBA title would answer all the many questions. But that just wasn't the case.

Magic Johnson had pulled his hamstring in the midst of the 1989 Finals, which helped Detroit to a 4-0 sweep of the championship.

Asked his perspective on the outcome, Boston Celtics President Red Auerbach quipped, "You gotta be lucky."

And that was the prevailing view of the Pistons. They had been lucky in 1989, their critics said. So instead of glorying in their title, they were faced

with proving themselves all over again.

And worse, they were forced to do so without Rick Mahorn. Right in the midst of their 1989 celebration, they had lost everybody's favorite power forward in the expansion draft.

It was a bad scene.

'Horn, as you may know, had been the ultimate Bad Boy. He sported a loud, profane exterior, which he used to police the team both on the court and in the locker room. But for the most part, his menacing countenance was just an act, which he often softened with a playful smile. Beneath the facade, Mahorn was a sweetheart. To the fans, children and adults alike, he offered a personal touch that many pro athletes didn't have. Beyond that, the coaches loved him. General Manager Jack McCloskey and the Pistons staff had guided him through a weight problem when he first came to the team in 1985. They had been positive and encouraging in his development as a player. In return, Mahorn had been fiercely loyal to the organization. He had often said publicly that he would run through a wall for Chuck Daly.

The bad news came during the Piston victory parade. At exactly the same time, the Minnesota Timberwolves were preparing to take Mahorn in the expansion draft. Working a portable phone from his float in the parade, McCloskey had tried frantically to work a deal. He offered guard Michael Williams and a first-round pick to the Timberwolves if they wouldn't take Mahorn. For a time, it appeared possible.

After the parade, the team held one final rally at the Palace before a throng of their most loyal fans. With the music blaring, the crowd watched replays of Finals highlights. Then the

Like Isiah, Mahorn was a leader.

lights went down, and a ballboy charged into the spotlight bearing the Bad Boys Skull 'n Crossbones flag. One by one, the players and coaches stepped into the spotlight and addressed the crowd.

McCloskey was first. "When I first came here," the general manager told the gathering, "everybody said the Pistons were losers. The players were losers. The coaches were losers. The front office people were losers. I say this to you. Sometimes winners are losers who just won't quit!"

In turn, each of the players came forward with messages that were met with blasts of noise and emotion from the crowd. Isiah stood at the mike and applauded the fans, who quickly returned the compliment. Next Dennis Rodman attempted to talk but found himself sobbing. Life really can be that sweet at times, and the Worm has no fear of acknowledging it. Isiah got up and hugged him. As they went to their seats, Mahorn led the fans in another round of Bad Boys chants. The crowd then calmed for him to speak, and he stepped over to shake Daly's hand.

"Thank you for having faith in me," he told his coach, then turned back to the crowd. "I'd like to thank God and my family," he said and grinned. "I'm glad to be the Baddest Boy you've ever seen."

The crowd screamed wildly and then quieted when Mahorn walked over to McCloskey. "I'd like to thank Jack McCloskey," he said. "Thank you for sticking with me through my weight problem."

Moments later, the proceedings closed in an outpouring of emotion, and the Pistons retreated to their locker room. Mahorn was still tingling from the experience when a sober-faced McCloskey asked him to step into the coaches' room. Inside, he found Daly and his assistants looking just as glum.

Like the other players, Mahorn had known that the Pistons would have to leave one of their top nine players unprotected in the draft. He had wondered briefly if he might be the one. But he had figured not. After all,

Aguirre had things to prove.

9

Mahorn was devastated, but he kept his composure. He spoke briefly with his teammates, told them he had enjoyed playing with them and wished them luck. At first, they thought he was joking.

he was a starter and an important part of the team.

But as soon as he stepped into the room and saw their expressions, he knew. They told him that they were sorry, that they had tried to strike a deal but that Minnesota wouldn't go for it.

Mahorn was devastated, but he kept his composure. He spoke briefly with his teammates, told them he had enjoyed playing with them and wished them luck. At first, they thought he was joking. But his face confirmed that he wasn't. In shock, Mahorn then left, stopping to sign an autograph on the way out.

"It was one of those days you don't want to think about, but something that will always stay with you," he said later. "It was miserable."

"It's a sad, sad day," McCloskey told the beat writers who had gathered around him for an explanation. "We feel like we're being penalized for having depth. It's heartbreaking."

Understandably bitter, Mahorn refused to report to the Timberwolves until his contract was renegotiated, so Minnesota sought to trade him. The Lakers wanted him badly, but a deal couldn't be arranged. Finally, in late October, the Timberwolves sent him to Philadelphia, which only increased the Pistons' anguish. Not only had they lost an intimidating player, but he would now make one of their Eastern Conference opponents much tougher. In Philly, Mahorn was given a new contract and teamed with small forward Charles Barkley to give the 76ers a surprisingly strong and intimidating frontcourt. The Sixers' marketing guys packaged them as

Scott Hastings was signed to bolster the frontcourt.

Spider started the season with new muscle.

Having witnessed one championship, the fans wanted another.

"Thump and Bump," which was as accurate as it was catchy. The Sixers would gain power as the season progressed, and that only increased speculation over whether Detroit had given up the wrong guy.

The Pistons, meanwhile, were left looking for a replacement at power forward. Plus, Chuck Daly wanted to identify a fourth guard and spent training camp looking at a variety of young prospects. Reggie Fox, Fennis Dembo, Lorenzo Sutton and Stan Kimbrough all battled for the open guard spot, but none of them wound up sticking with the team.

McCloskey bolstered the frontcourt by signing veteran forwards Scott Hastings and David Greenwood, but the starting power forward job remained a question mark. McCloskey had also obtained rookie forward Anthony Cook from Phoenix, but he was considered a developmental project and signed to play in Greece. "Cook isn't ready to contribute right now," McCloskey said. "He could be great down the road."

Just like any mature pro team, the Pistons' future was now. They needed a power forward that could help them win another title. One of last year's bench players would have to emerge. John Salley was the leading candidate and wanted the job. He had lifted weights over the summer and added muscle to his lanky seven-foot frame. "I like starting," he said. "I like making an impact at the start." But Daly viewed him as better suited to playing off the bench. Salley's shotblocking presence was great for shifting momentum when he went into games. Daly wanted to search around the roster a bit for a new combination. Whatever he would decide, the coach didn't seem openly distressed about it. He had talked to John Madden over the summer and asked the former Oakland Raiders coach how he prepared his team after its Super Bowl success. Madden told him it was important not to try to defend the title in training camp, that the pressures of repeating as

Even the V.P. joined the Bad Boys in '90.

Worm and Spider played well together.

champions should be avoided. Don't worry about winning the championship until you've earned your way into the playoffs, Madden said.

That seemed like good advice, Daly thought. He wanted camp to be what it had always been—the place where he determined who would earn playing time. It would be the place where he would find a power forward and a fourth guard, or so he hoped.

"Camp is where it counts," the coach said confidently as the session opened. "These things kind of weed themselves out."

But the weeding wasn't immediate. The Pistons got off to a so-so start in the exhibition season, and quickly found the world was waiting in ambush. They had expected to be jostled during their World Championship tour that fall, but not so early and so often.

Their first scrap came in an October 17 exhibition game in Roanoke, Virginia, against Seattle. The Sonics were ready from the start. "It was an incredibly physical game," Daly said afterward. "I mean it was like the Finals. They came out and played the hell out of the game."

Reserve center Williams Bedford hit a late free throw to give Detroit a 99-98 win.

"I have a feeling it's something we're going to face every night," Daly said.

A week later, the players got their first look at their championship rings, which would be presented at the first home game of the regular season, against New York on November 3. Each 14-carat gold ring sported eight diamonds and was valued at more than $4,000. Inside was inscribed

Daly loves a blue suit.

"Bad Boys, Detroit 4, Los Angeles 0."

"You get a little chill when you see them," Mark Aguirre said. "This is what you play in this league for. Only a privileged few get one of these."

The hope of getting a ring had made Aguirre eager to come to the Pistons from Dallas in the February 1989 trade for Adrian Dantley. Several writers, most of whom had known Aguirre in the Western Conference, had predicted that he

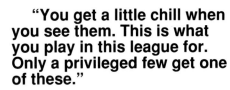

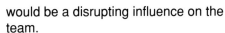

"You get a little chill when you see them. This is what you play in this league for. Only a privileged few get one of these."

—Mark Aguirre

Aguirre came into camp in shape.

would be a disrupting influence on the team.

Sure, he had behaved while the Pistons won their first championship, a Western Conference beat writer said the night after the 1989 Finals. "But next year, after he's gotten a ring, he'll be a pig." It was an opinion held by many observers.

Which made Aguirre yet another question mark for the Pistons in the fall of 1989. Would he continue to find satisfaction merely as a team player in Detroit? Or would he play the pig?

Aguirre had begun answering that question early. His weight had bloated to 253 pounds during the '89 Finals, but he reported to camp 90 days later with 29 pounds trimmed from his girth. He was svelte and pleasant and seemed eager to do whatever was asked of him. Even so, people still had their doubts.

"He came here last year, but he wasn't really acclimated to the way we operate here," Laimbeer told columnist Bryan Burwell of The Detroit News. "The heat is still on him. He knows he is one of the guys who will always have to prove himself. He has a label that probably won't ever go away. The bottom line is that you're not a Detroit Piston simply because you're ON the Detroit Pistons. That's something you have to earn."

As it turned out, Aguirre didn't have to provide the controversy early in the season. Jack McCloskey took care of that by offering Atlanta free agent Jon Koncak a $2.6 million, one-year contract. The high offer for a player with such a journeyman's abilities infuriated the Hawks, as well

Buddha opened the year in a slump but soon got it together.

Dumars' role in the offense expanded.

as other teams around the league. Atlanta bettered Detroit's offer by giving the seven-foot Koncak an astounding six-year contract worth a reported $13.2 million, a move that wracked the Hawks roster with dissension. Koncak was making plenty more than several of his more talented teammates. Atlanta would sputter through the season, and much of the blame for their performance would go to their payroll problems.

Atlanta Coach Mike Fratello went so far as to accuse McCloskey of making the offer to disrupt the Hawks. "They knew what they were doing," Fratello said of Pistons management.

McCloskey denied it. "We wanted Jon Koncak," he said.

As it turned out, the Pistons found their frontcourt answer right where Daly hoped they would. In his one and a half seasons with the Pistons, veteran center James Edwards had started only one game. At 7'1", Edwards had always shown an ability to score throughout his 12-year pro career. But his defensive intensity was suspect, so Daly had used him whenever the team needed a jolt of low-post offense.

But with Mahorn's departure, the pressure had increased on Edwards. Many observers had figured that the team would give him up in the expansion draft rather than his close friend Mahorn. Perhaps because of this pressure, Edwards had come into camp with more intensity and had played better.

When the Pistons headed west for a two-game series with Phoenix toward the close of the exhibition season, Daly decided to start Edwards for the second time in his Pistons career. He responded by scoring 23 points, and although the Pistons lost, Daly was obviously pleased.

"He got the start because I thought he deserved it," the coach told Drew Sharp of the Free Press. "I wanted to take a look at him and see what he could do. He's been pretty consistent offensively and he's been working on his defense."

But rather than settle on Edwards

early, Daly went on to take a full look at his options. If nothing else, the loss of Mahorn demonstrated how fragile the chemistry of a championship team really is. As the coaching staff searched for answers, the roster seemed in disarray. Vinnie Johnson was hampered by a broken left rib. Both Joe Dumars and Isiah weren't shooting well. And in the frontcourt, Salley and Rodman struggled.

Part of the problem with the offense was the intensity of opposing defenses. Everywhere the Pistons went they found a team eager to gun them down. Even Daly was surprised by it. "None of us has gone through defending a championship and facing what we have to face every night," he said. "You talk about it, but you have to be able to see what's going on. I don't know if everybody can play this way every night, but that's what is happening."

That intensity jumped a notch in the final exhibition game, against the 76ers at the Skydome in Toronto. Neither Barkley nor Mahorn played for Philadelphia, but the meeting still had plenty of zing. With about six minutes to go in a close game, Edwards and Philly center Mike Gminski got into a scuffle. Then Isiah dragged Gminski backward, and all three were ejected. About two minutes later, Daly drew his second technical for arguing a call and got the heave-ho. With assistant Brendan Suhr running the show, they still won, 107-98, to finish the exhibition season at 5-3. But more important than wins or losses they had gotten an understanding of what they faced.

"A lot of teams are coming after us because we don't have Rick," Edwards told Terry Foster of the News. "They think we won't stand up. If we allow them to crack us, then

Laimbeer's game just got better.

19

Every opponent seemed ready to scuffle.

they will crack us the entire game. We have to stand up for ourselves."

In the wake of the warlike exhibition season, Daly called for a new strategy: non-violence. "We should maintain a Gandhi-like demeanor and turn the other cheek," he said. "If teams are going to try and do this, then we've got to keep our heads together and stay in the game."

Around the league, opponents chuckled at such a notion. They remembered well the Bad Boys menace from the previous season, and most of them had decided to fight fire with fire. Even Daly's troops gave a smile at his call for peace. "We expect this kind of stuff to keep happening," the Worm told Drew Sharp of the *Free Press.* "But we're not going to change the way we play."

ADJUSTMENTS TO MAKE

So they entered the regular season, a bit intimidated, shooting poorly, and unsure of their starting frontcourt. Management made the final cuts on November 1, keeping Stan Kimbrough, a slight rookie guard out of Xavier, as the 12th man, but he would stay with the team only until McCloskey could find a veteran backup.

The uncertainty over the upcoming schedule was eased somewhat by the ring ceremony that Friday night, November 3. After all, they were the defending World Champions, and that brought an immense amount of confidence. Dumars, though, thought they should quickly forget their past accomplishments. "We've got a new season and a new challenge to think about," he said. "We were the champions last season. This is an entirely new beginning."

They got things started right that night, first raising their championship banner, then beating the Knicks, 106-103, with clutch defensive play late in the game. Dumars emerged from a mini-slump to score 26 points, but as he pointed out afterward, it was the work at the other end of the floor that did the trick.

"Our style hasn't changed," he

Laimbeer gets Ewing's attention.

Isiah and Aguirre, two old pals, confer.

21

said. "If we're to win, we've got to do it on the defensive end."

Daly settled on Salley as the starting power forward, and he responded with three blocked shots and good play.

There was no rest, though. The next night they played the first of a five-game road trip. In all, 17 of Detroit's first 27 games would be away. Before Christmas, they would complete two West-Coast circuits, all of which left Daly telling anyone who would listen that it was the toughest schedule he had ever seen.

They seemed strangely complacent the next night in Washington, but after waiting on his teammates, Zeke finally took over in the second half, scoring 20 points as they got a second win, 95-93.

Then they went to Chicago, where the Bulls whacked 'em with a couple of late buckets, 117-114. The Bulls had lost their previous seven home games to the Pistons, but Detroit gave up 70 points in the second half to help them end the streak.

Indianapolis served the next notice. Detroit scored 13 points in the first quarter, 12 in the second, the total of 25 points being the lowest scoring half in team history. The Pistons tried to win by shooting jumpers and their field goal percentage plunged into the 30s. The Pacers strode easily, 95-74.

"It was an embarrassment," the Worm said afterward.

And it would get worse.

Two nights later, they beat the Orlando Magic, but then they fumbled late against the Miami Heat and lost 88-84.

It was the worst game he had seen in seven years as Pistons coach, Daly said. "We're struggling, and we'll keep struggling until we get back the killer instinct."

They returned home with a 3-3 record and seemed stuck in their funk at Monday's practice. Finally, Daly walked onto the floor to end the session. But the players waved him off. They wanted to keep working until they got it right. "We're going to get through this," Salley allowed.

Part of the problem was the once-

Aguirre boosted the offense.

Things weren't easy in the fall.

22

The coaches juggled the lineup early.

Laimbeer was the epitome of a Piston.

Dumars shook off an early slump.

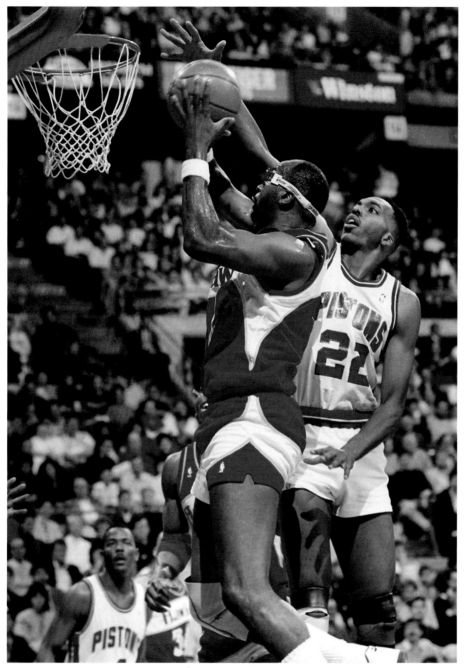

The Hawks ended Detroit's 25-game home win streak.

the Palace; the Pistons hadn't lost a regular-season game there since January 27, 1989. But the Hawks ended that streak later in the week, 103-96. "We didn't play with any emotion or intensity," Laimbeer said. "And when that happens, we're going to get tagged."

They had been tagged four times in the first eight games of the season. Always a gourmet worrier, Daly suddenly had real reasons for concern. Following the Atlanta game, they beat Cleveland, then headed west again for a five-game slate that began in Portland on Sunday night, November 26. The Pistons hadn't won there since October 19, 1974, 19 straight losses.

They opened their road trip by making it 20 straight. Even worse, they fell hard, 102-82.

"This club could win 55 games," Brendan Suhr said of the Blazers. Portland had outrebounded the Pistons, 58-44. Detroit, meanwhile, continued to go for long jumpers. Vinnie, Zeke and Joe hit just nine of their 36 shots.

The Blazers, on the other hand, were eager to prove something. "We wanted to make a statement," Portland coach Rick Adelman said. "We wanted to show we could play with a team the caliber of the world champions."

The Blazers had done that, and they would do it again.

For the Pistons, the situation wasn't exactly desperate. But it was enough to generate sleeplessness. Afterward, at their hotel, Isiah and Daly talked about the team's options until 3 a.m. Something needed to be done, the coach finally decided. Power foward remained the problem area. Salley hadn't done a bad job as a starter, averaging about eight points and six rebounds over 27 minutes each game. But the Pistons seemed slow getting started offensively each game, and the bench was in disarray.

So Daly decided to shift Salley to the bench and start Edwards, something of a surprise in that Edwards had been in a terrible shooting slump over the first 10 games. "Buddha," though, had

strong bench. The reserves had been outscored in four games. Figuring he could step up the bench's scoring punch, Aguirre offered to give up his starting role to Rodman. The Worm appreciated the gesture but declined.

While he was still trying to settle on a rotation, Daly wanted the team to take better shots. Always a perimeter team, the Pistons were relying ever increasingly on long-range solutions. They weren't going to the hole enough. Even worse, Edwards had fallen into a terrible slump, hitting just 30 percent of his shots. His low-post

scoring off the bench was vital to Detroit's offensive efficiency.

They righted themselves a bit by going to their old stand-by: defense. The Celtics came into town November 18 with a full head of early-season steam, but Detroit knocked 'em down quickly. The Pistons forced 21 turnovers in the first half and held Boston to just 39 points. The result was a 103-86 blowout that boosted the stat sheet. Detroit shot 47 percent from the floor and had just five turnovers.

It was the 25th consecutive win in

maintained that his numbers would improve. And Daly believed him. But more important, Daly wanted Salley to make the bench the weapon it had been the previous season. In announcing the move to the beat writers, Daly emphasized that it was not a demotion. He informed Salley of the change when the team arrived at its hotel in Sacramento for the next stop. Salley took it in his rather large stride.

"The more we win, the better we'll be," he said.

Across the roster, the Pistons were edgy. Vinnie Johnson became uncharacteristically vocal in practice. He yelled and exhorted his teammates and even did a little coaching. "I just think we need some leadership," the Microwave explained.

Laimbeer, meanwhile, called for an end to any Gandhi-like play. "Teams are coming after us, and it's going to be mean ugly basketball," he predicted. "You are going to have to step up and be a man. We've got to go out there and hit people and fight for rebounds. When a guy is coming in the lane or going for a rebound, you've got to tag him."

The shift and the emotion began working immediately for the 7-5 Pistons. They won at Sacramento and then headed to Phoenix. Salley and Rodman reunited to bring a gusto to the bench play. "We're like Mutt and Jeff," the Worm said. "I don't think one can be effective without the other."

Vinnie, as well, welcomed "Spider" back to the second unit. After all, their brand of mayhem had stirred fear in opponents for three years.

For old time's sake, they gave the Suns a taste of it on November 29 and got another road win, 111-103, as Salley scored 15. Isiah did his part with 29 points, 14 assists and nine rebounds. And Laimbeer scored 21 with 13 rebounds, then took a bow as the Phoenix fans vehemently booed him at the end of the game. The Bad Boys, it seemed, were back, and just in the nick of time. Their next stop was the Forum, and the Los Angeles press was making plenty of noise about the previous year's Finals being just a fluke. At game time that

Friday, a couple of Laker fans greeted the Pistons with a banner: "How do the Pistons spell NBA Championship? HAMSTRINGS."

They spelled WIN the same old way, though. Detroit matched the Lakers in regulation, then held them scoreless in overtime, the first time a team had been shut out in overtime since 1983.

Salley had badly wanted to be a starter, but three straight road victories convinced him that he was more valuable coming off the bench. "I know all that matters is winning," he said. "We're a better team now than we were a few days ago."

Salley and Rodman reunited to bring a gusto to the bench play. "We're like Mutt and Jeff," the Worm told the writers. "I don't think one can be effective without the other."

They didn't show it the next night, though. A quick trip up the coast to Seattle produced only a 120-95 loss. "We were just a game away from our best game of the season, then we played our worst," observed Rodman, who was ejected after drawing two technicals.

They headed home with a 10-6 record and weren't really displeased with their 3-2 showing on the trip. Part

of the reason for their outlook was Edwards' play. In his first eight games as a starter, he shot 53 percent from the floor and hit a string of 21 consecutive free throws. Suddenly the Pistons had a force in the low post.

Three days later, McCloskey settled the fourth guard issue on December 5 by signing veteran guard Gerald Henderson, who had been waived by Milwaukee. He had played a major role in Boston's 1984 championship, and his experience was considered a plus. Some observers speculated that Henderson might take an even larger role with Vinnie slogging his way through a slump.

"Vinnie is the guy we're going to play, no matter what," Daly told the beat writers. "I can live with his shooting slump, but it's important he do the other things."

They beat Washington at home (Laimbeer had 23 rebounds and 29 points), then headed to Philadelphia for their reunion with Mahorn. The writers suggested the meeting might be a brawl.

"It won't feel strange hitting each other," Laimbeer replied when asked about Mahorn. "It'll be just like practice used to be. But when he tags us coming down the lane, Rickey will just smile and keep on playing."

True to the forecasts, there was trouble. Isiah and Mahorn tangled. And the Sixers won, 107-101, breaking Philadelphia's eight-game losing streak to Detroit. Mahorn scored 22 points and had 14 rebounds. "It was a very emotional night for me," he said afterward.

Detroit recovered with a big home win over the division-leading Indiana Pacers, 121-93. Isiah scored 30 points. "It seems like when I play hard and aggressive, the rest of the team follows suit," he observed afterward.

And when he was down, the Pistons struggled. They began a four-game, five-night western road trip after the Indiana win. The tour opened in Denver, where the Pistons promptly fell behind by 16. At halftime, Thomas sulked alone by

Spider became a better banger.

Buddha's defense improved.

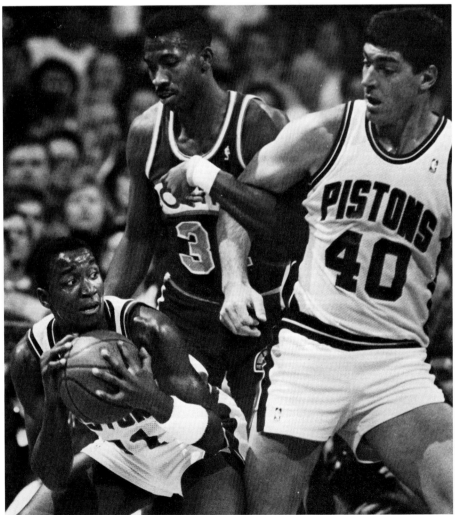

Isiah and Bill locked up the Sonics.

Joe goes for the assist against Seattle.

himself in a corner of the locker room, which irked Laimbeer.

"Where are you at?" he asked. "The rest of us are busting our butts."

Thomas said he would take care of business. And he did, scoring 24 points in the second half to lead the comeback win, 121-108.

"We have to get on his stuff just like everybody else," explained Aguirre, who scored 29. "We jumped on him, hollered at him. But he takes it."

But by no means was Isiah cured of what ailed him. They played poorly in a December 13 loss to the Clippers during which Thomas screamed at official Don Vaden and was ejected. Isiah had shot 27 percent from the floor during the game, and his frustration built until Laimbeer had to pull him away from Vaden.

"Don't ever do that again, or I'll kick your butt," Zeke told his center.

Two nights later against Utah, Isiah suffered a concussion when he caught an elbow from Jazz guard John Stockton. The Pistons went on to lose 94-91. Afterward, they flew to Oakland to play Golden State, and upon their arrival Thomas was hospitalized overnight while his teammates lost to the Warriors.

Detroit had become the Sad Boys instead of the Bad Boys, wrote the *San Francisco Examiner's* Art Spander. "One fourth into the season, this Pistons edition is only a pathetic reminder of what it used to be."

"Every town we've been in, they keep writing that we're not playing like the defending champions," Daly told Spander. "What does that mean? This is a new year, not last year. Eleven out of the last 14 games have been on the road.

"It's always like a dream, winning a championship. You see somebody else do it, and you keep wishing that somebody was you. Then you win it and find there are new problems. But I'll tell you, they're all worth it."

Even better, Daly said, he could now look down the road and see promise. "We're going to be playing a lot of home games. I feel good about my club."

The Pistons could now reap the

benefits of a tough early schedule. They returned home at 14-10, got three days rest and then repaid Seattle, 94-77. Isiah came back from injury but missed all 10 shots he took from the floor.

They followed that with a tough win at New Jersey and a home victory over Orlando. Their reward

"One fourth into the season, this Pistons edition is only a pathetic reminder of what it used to be."

—Art Spander

was three badly needed days off at Christmas, which refreshed them enough to get a treasured road win over Cleveland on December 27. Buddha scored a season-high 25 points and shot 66 percent from the floor. Edwards as a starter had been a tremendous boost.

"We're kind of riding him a little bit," Daly said.

The win, their fourth straight, left them 17-10, a half game out of the Central Division lead. They were beginning to feel their oats. Practices got rougher. They talked more trash. With most of their

games at home and given the Christmas break, they were rested.

The only weary soul seemed to be Isiah, who had taken a knee in the thigh against Cleveland. The season's early pressure and the injuries had taken their toll on the team captain. He was edgy. Aguirre thought he needed a break and said so. Since his concussion at Utah, his scoring had dropped from 19 points to 12 points per game. *Free Press* columnist Charlie Vincent asked what was wrong.

Nothing, Isiah told him. Things will work out.

Vincent took his question to Chuck Daly. "He's just going through one of those stretches that every player goes through," Daly said. "And don't forget the burden he carries, being the leader of this club on the floor and in the locker room. This is his franchise. This is his city. He has made this franchise."

That Friday, December 29, they lost their second game of the season in the Palace. Isiah made only one of eight from the field as Milwuakee won, 99-85.

The next night, they closed out 1989 on a power failure. Two pre-game outages plunged the Palace and 15,000 fans into darkness. The lights came back on after a 23-minute delay, and the Pistons beat New Jersey in a game highlighted by the Worm's running half-court bucket at the end of the first quarter.

"I was surprised it went in," Rodman said. "I just wanted to get it out of my hands."

They finished November and December at 18-11, certainly not a world championship pace but not bad for a team that had made two West Coast trips.

A HAPPY NEW YEAR

The new calendar unfolded like Chuck Daly's dream book. In a show of power, they beat Orlando, the Clippers, Indiana, New York and Chicago to go 5-0 over the first nine days of 1990. During that time, Laimbeer, Thomas, Aguirre and Dumars took turns leading the

Zeke seldom let up.

Jordan continued to be a problem for Detroit.

Trainer Mike works on Dumars' hamstring.

scoring. When they were finished they had moved into first place in the Central Division by half a game.

Against Chicago, Dumars had been the spearhead in a 100-90 win, holding Michael Jordan to 16 points while scoring 28 himself.

"He's an exceptional player," Super Mike said of Joe afterward.

"Broadway Joe!" Salley hooted at Dumars in the locker room.

Salley's smile was bigger than his Detroit mansion. He had reason to be upbeat. He had shut down one of Jordan's drives with a stupendous block. "We are in a groove right now," he said. "Everybody seems to know their role. We're enjoying playing."

"I like our team and where we're headed," Isiah declared. "Our ship is straight."

But then on the tenth day of 1990, it sailed into Boston harbor, which was bad timing. The night before the Celtics had lost to New Jersey in a game that featured a six-point Boston quarter, the lowest total in their substantial history. They compensated by stopping Detroit, 104-97.

"Tonight was a great basketball game," Celtics coach Jimmy Rodgers allowed afterward.

The Pistons hardly saw it that way. They felt the officials had allowed Robert Parish and Kevin McHale to set up residence in the lane. That damage inside killed them.

Fortunately, the Bad Boys had a knack for forgetting quickly. They returned home and claimed wins over Minnesota and Portland. But then they went back to Philly and lost again to Thump and Bump. Barkley had 30.

Back at home, they coasted past Golden State on January 19, as Dumars scored 30. Afterward, Aguirre noticed Edwards slipping his championship ring onto his finger.

"Buddha's going out tonight," Aguirre announced to the locker room. "He's wearing his ring."

Edwards responded with a sly, knowing smile. Yes, he was dressed to the nines and headed for a night out. And, yes, he was sporting the gold. It was amazing what a

difference a championship ring had made in his life. Just a few years ago, Edwards was an aging journeyman center cast off by the Pheonix Suns for next to nothing. But now he had become an integral part of a world championship team.

Which meant that he could wear the ring, that glistening glob of gold and diamonds. For the Bad Boys,

success had been a bit gaudy. But the very fact that Edwards was sporting his ring raised the major question now facing the Pistons— would one ring be enough? Or would their futures be gaudier still?

They scoffed at the mention of pressure, but that question had left the team toiling in an air of uneasiness. They had been tight-

You make the call.

Team defense was their specialty.

Aguirre even learned to like defense a bit.

lipped with the press and edgy over the first three months of the season. They seemed caught in an identity crisis. In 1989, they had been the Darth Vaders, the hard-foul pirates of the NBA. For 1990, the Bad Boys banner still flew in the rafters at the Palace, Laimbeer still gave a hack or two, and the Palace sound system continued to blare out George Thorogood's "Bad to the Bone." But without Mahorn, the Pistons were nowhere near as Bad as before. By February of 1989, the Bad Boys had already been fined $24,500 by the league's front office for fighting, fouling and general mayhem. At the same point in the 1990 season, they had racked up only $2,500 in fighting fines, hardly a respectable figure for a team that prided itself on intimidation.

As much as anyone, Isiah had felt the frustration of Mahorn's loss. For seven years, Thomas and the organization had worked to build a championship club. "People look back on last year's team and realize that it was one of the greatest teams in the history of sports," he said the next day after practice. "You can compare it to the Chicago Bears team of 1985. The things that we did to win, people don't necessarily understand yet. But I think two, three, four years from now, people will look back and start patterning their teams after us."

Yet just when the building job was completed, the NBA's expansion had cost the Pistons the opportunity for real greatness. "Expansion has hurt us," Thomas said, "but it's also hurt just about every other team. Now,

there are no more dominant teams in the league. Last year we were a dominant team. Had we been able to keep our team together we would have still been a dominant team... We could have won three out of the next four years.

"We're capable of winning it this year. But you look at next year and the year after. Those are question marks because this team's getting a little older. The older guys are having to play more minutes. Therefore you don't have the luxury of having them for four years. You burn them out in two. That's the problem you've got."

All of this talk of aging made Thomas sound a lot like the Celtics and Lakers, which was exactly how he wanted to sound. "The Lakers had tradition," he said. "The Celtics had tradition. They could be themselves. We, as the Detroit Pistons, needed a gimmick, a hook, to get people to respect us. People never respected the Detroit Pistons. Even the officials didn't respect us."

The Bad Boys identity had become that necessary gimmick for respect, but it had outlived its usefulness. At least in Isiah's mind.

"Having won the championship, we don't need hooks now," he said. "We don't need gimmicks."

Even if Jack McCloskey could retrace his steps and magically bring Mahorn back to the Pistons, it wouldn't work, Isiah said. "It can never be the same again. It's like when a singer makes a record, like when Michael Jackson cut 'Billy Jean.' All of the remakes of that song were different and were never the same. There could never be another 'Billy Jean,' just like there can only be one Bad Boys team. Even if you went back and got Mahorn, it could never be the same. That's just how life goes."

So the Pistons had set out to cut a new groove. And Thomas knew that would take time. The Pistons weren't the Bad Boys they had been, and their new identity was not complete. "We have yet to find ourselves, or find what this team is capable of doing," he said. "Over the course of the regular season, we're practicing and

Magic came to the Palace with determination.

> **For his part, Daly didn't want to discard the Bad Boys motif. Still, he was having fun watching this new identity unfold.**

experimenting to get ready for the playoffs. The main point is to develop as a playoff team. This team won't fully develop its personality, we won't find what we're capable of doing until March."

For his part, Daly didn't want to discard the Bad Boys motif. Still, he was having fun watching this new identity unfold. Asked what he perceived as the difference in his 1990 team, the coach replied, "We're physical, but not as physical."

Surprisingly, they played better defense. In 1989, they gave up 101 points per game on the average. For 1990, they allowed opponents only 98.3 per outing. The explanation was simple, Daly said. Their success in the 1989 playoffs had made the Pistons real believers in defense. And with Mahorn gone, Rodman, the defensive whiz, was seeing more playing time.

Just as surprisingly, the Pistons were scoring less in 1990—102 points per game as opposed to 106 for 1989. But that could partly be explained in the newfound efficiency in their halfcourt game. With Edwards scoring down low, the offense was controlling the clock more. "We've changed up front," Daly said. "Jimmy is playing very very well in the low post, scoring great, because he's getting a lot more minutes."

Everyone on the roster could sense this new identity building. They weren't as Bad, weren't as loud, weren't as brash.

"We realize it's not about talking, it's about playing," Salley said.

So they really were the new low-key Pistons? he was asked.

"Low key, yeah," he said. "Low key in first place."

The Pistons and Lakers had a physical meeting in January.

STREAKIN'

Their eyes, of course, had been cast across the continent, out to Magic Land, where the Lakers possessed the league's best record. That top spot might have seemed comfortable for Pat Riley's crew, except that Los Angeles had lost seven straight games to Detroit, running back through the '89 Finals. The dominant team of the '80s had suddenly found themselves psyched by the Pistons. They didn't like it, and showed as much when they came to the Palace on January 21.

When they appeared for pre-game warmups, Magic paused a moment at the head of the Laker layup line. His game face affixed, he worked his gum nervously, then sighed, took a deep breath and headed off toward the basket. He wanted this one badly. Riley did, too, and had worked them over psychologically to get ready for it.

Minutes later, with the Palace music loud and the fans settling into their seats, Magic waited by the Laker bench, eager for things to get started. He turned away from the floor, closed his eyes, and exhaled slowly. Then the official came over with the game ball. Magic checked it out, bouncing it three quick times and nodding his approval.

The crescendo of the introductions followed. Noise. Horns. Music. He pitched his gum under the bench. Eased his knee guards into place.

Adjusted his socks. Tugged at his shorts. Magic was ready.

Or so he thought.

Edwards worked the post early for Detroit, and the Pistons took a 7-0 lead. Then it grew to 11-2. Riley, however, remained composed, arms folded, pacing the sideline. From the very start, the battling under the boards had been furious. The Pistons seemed to be winning it. Finally at 6:58, the Laker coach called a timeout and took a knee in front of his bench, raising his finger instructively to make a point.

Things continued to worsen for Los Angeles, and two minutes later, Riley called on Michael Cooper to replace Magic, who was nervous and tight and struggling. Ninety seconds later, Daly countered with Rodman.

Like that, the game shifted gears and went to a new level. By the start of the second period, Daly had fully deployed the Pistons Dream Team—Rodman, Salley, Vinnie, Laimbeer and Dumars—what some observers called Detroit's best lineup. They promptly took over. Salley went baseline on Vlade Divac and forced the Lakers' rookie center into his second foul. Then Vinnie scored to give Detroit a 28-17 lead. The Lakers looked to their trapping defense, and moments later Cooper, his arms raised like a wall, had Vinnie pinned against the far right sideline. Vinnie rose up and launched a trey.

As it fell, Riley, standing at midcourt, exclaimed in anguish, turned to his bench and half laughed. Things didn't look good for ending Detroit's streak. Yet somehow, behind Worthy's scoring, Los Angeles stayed close. And at the 7:34 mark of the second period, with the Lakers trailing 37-28, Riley decided that Magic had had plenty of time to observe the game during his long rest.

"Buck," he called.

The bench having done its job, Magic returned rested and calmed. He promptly got an assist on a Worthy bucket and the lead was 37-30.

The first half developed into a Worthy/Edwards contest. Neither team could stop the other's big scorer. With three minutes to go in the second quarter, Buddha hit again, giving him 19 points. Meanwhile, Byron Scott and Mychal Thompson still hadn't scored. Regardless, the Lakers kept trapping and working at the Detroit lead.

Late in the half, Aguirre hit a trey, putting the Pistons up, 51-45. Then back at the other end, he concentrated on defending Worthy, perhaps focusing harder on defense than he ever had in his life. It didn't matter. Worthy quickly flashed right, then zoomed left into the lane, tossing up a finger roll from eight feet. It was a soft swish, 51-47.

Zeke had seemed weary in December and early January.

Worthy and Aguirre went down in the third quarter.

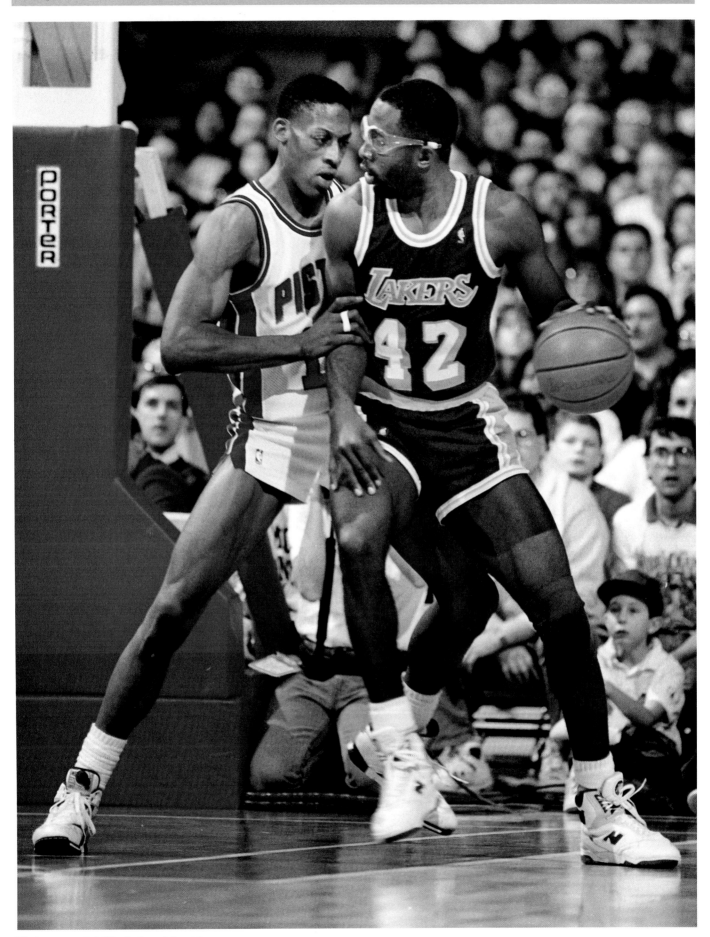

Worm can match Worthy's quickness.

Laimbeer and Magic squared off.

Dumars took Magic to the hole next to move it to 53-47, but just before the buzzer A.C. Green knocked in a three-pointer to make the halftime lead 53-50. The Pistons knew they were in trouble. They had played well for a half, hitting unbelievable shots and holding the Laker guards in the miserable range. Even after doing all of this, Detroit led by only three.

The Lakers quickly eliminated that in the third period. Green scored first, then Scott finally contributed with a three-pointer to give Los Angeles the lead, 55-53. Detroit called a 20-second timeout, but Scott scored again seconds later to put the Lakers up, 57-53. Edwards, meanwhile, was closed down by Mychal Thompson, who forced him away from the basket.

The Laker lead grew, and then Aguirre went down. He was driving to the basket when Worthy went across his body to block his shot. They both crashed to the floor in a heap under the basket. But play didn't stop. Both bodies were pulled from the playing area as the action raced the other way. Aguirre attempted to rise, then slumped again. He was later taken off in a neck brace, and the Laker onslaught continued.

With 3:32 left in the third, Los Angeles led, 71-61, and the Pistons seemed dazed. Then Laimbeer was knocked down by Magic. He got up and shoved the Laker guard, bringing everybody onto the court to calm things. The period ended with Los Angeles leading 80-69.

A lot of teams had allowed the Pistons to set perimeter picks and take their jumpers, but the Lakers

Laimbeer plays defense like a lumberjack.

were fighting through those picks, forcing the Pistons into a street scrap just to get their shots off. The play was very physical. To start the fourth period, the officials visited each huddle to explain what they wouldn't allow.

The Lakers pushed their margin to 83-69 early in the fourth, but five minutes later, the Pistons had cut it to 85-80 on Isiah's offensive rebound and stickback. The timing was right for a Detroit surge, but it would get no closer. Late in the game, in frustration, Isiah tapped Thompson's head with a flurry of punches and was ejected.

Moments later, the Lakers finished it, 105-97, and Riley strode down the sideline and gave Thompson a high slap of satisfaction. Thompson's excellent low-post defense on Edwards had been the crucial factor.

The Pistons were stunned. It wasn't the loss itself so much as it was the way they lost. They had been out-Badded by the Lakers, who had turned their act from Showtime to 'Bowtime. Los Angeles pushed and shoved and banged the Pistons out of the low post and out of the game. It was pure Malice in the Palace.

"Aggressiveness is defined as the disposition to dominate, and they have dominated us in the aggressiveness department," Riley said afterward. "They're used to playing that game." What the Lakers did to the Pistons was merely turn their own rough game upon them. Edwards had given the Pistons a new look in the low post, the kind of big-man scoring Detroit hadn't seen in years. But the Lakers simply shoved him out beyond his range and shut down the Pistons' halfcourt offense.

"They were sending people at me every time I got the ball," observed a weary Edwards.

Would the Lakers have been able to do that with Mahorn still around? Riley was asked.

Probably not, he replied. "But that's the way it goes, doesn't it? They had a choice to make [in leaving Mahorn unprotected for the expansion draft]. Rick's a great player. I tell you, he's making

By mid-season, Edwards was a force.

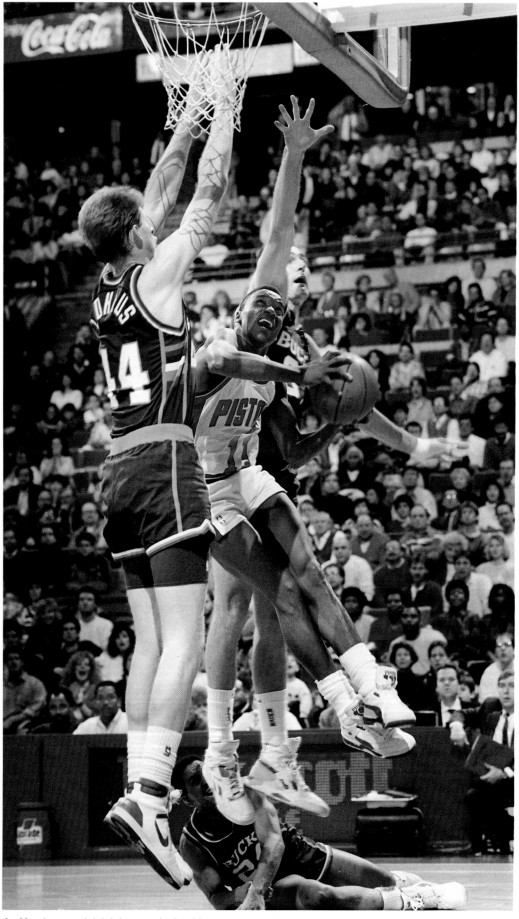

As March neared, Isiah began playing big.

Isiah and Joe had become the league's best set of guards.

Philadelphia this season. You can see the spirit of the 76ers change. We tried for three months to get Rick Mahorn in Los Angeles."

The Pistons still had their intimidating personality, Riley said, "but Rick was a big part of it. They miss him. They miss him a little bit."

Fortunately, the loss to the Lakers served to wake them, not shake them. Because they had won in 1989 on mental toughness as much as talent, they felt that same toughness would help them overcome the grueling process of repeating as champions.

Eventually it did.

They responded to the Laker loss by going on a 25-1 win streak, the third strongest in league history, stretching from January to March. With Aguirre out briefly with a concussion, Rodman moved into the

They responded to the Laker loss by going on a 25-1 win streak, the third strongest in league history, stretching from January to March.

starting lineup and stayed there, his defense and enthusiasm playing a major role in the team's blastoff.

Bolstering their play was a newfound confidence, which the Pistons toted everywhere they went around the league. The key, Salley said in the middle of the streak, "was being number one, knowing you're the only team that lasted number one until June, being the World Champions no matter where you go. We are a little more lax than last year. But I think we understand what it takes. We know how to win. We know how to lose also, which I think is a big thing. We don't let a loss take us deep down in the ground."

"You know where you're going," Isiah agreed. "You know the pitfalls. You know how to get up and you

Vinnie remained calm through his shooting troubles.

know not to be afraid."

Two nights after losing to the Lakers, they won in Chicago. Then they came back to the Palace and beat Phoenix with Laimbeer's 31 points and 23 rebounds. That was followed by road wins over Minnesota and Atlanta, a home win over Washington and another success in Cleveland. With their streak at seven games, people began noticing. Each successive win became more of a battle. Every team they met seemed ready to match the Pistons blow for blow.

"That takes a lot out of you," Salley said, "because everybody else is

playing real tough against us. Everybody else is trying to prove how tough they can be, how strong they can be."

They whipped Utah and Cleveland in the Palace and Milwaukee on the road to head into the All-Star break with a nine-game streak and a 35-14 record, one game ahead of the pace they had set in 1989 while racking up a team-record 63-win season.

Daly, Dumars, Thomas and Rodman went to Miami for the All-Star game, while everybody else rested. When the season resumed on February 13, Laimbeer had 20 rebounds in leading the Pistons to

Joe carried the offensive load many nights.

their 10th consecutive win, a 106-96 domination of Denver. After that, they beat Miami twice and then Orlando, 140-109.

But there came a time when even their mental toughness wasn't enough to get a win. "It's only so much that your body can take," Thomas said. "Sometimes you can say it's a matter of mind over matter. Sometimes your mind can be as strong as you want it to be, and your body will say, 'Hey, I got to stop and rest.' It's like a built-in clock that tells you your body can only take so much. And then you hit the wall.

"The key is if you can regroup as a team and go back at it again. Some teams hit the wall and never get up. You go at it as hard as you can, and when your body tells you you can't, you just lose that game. And you wake up the next morning and go on to the next one."

They rolled into Atlanta February 23 with a 13-game streak and promptly bottomed out, losing 112-103. Two nights later, they regrouped for a win in New York as Dumars scored 31. Back in the Palace on the 27th, they needed an overtime and a game-saving block from Rodman to beat Houston. Isiah scored 37 and had 10 assists.

Their streak went to 16-1 with a road win in Washington. Then they took on Philadelphia in the Palace again, and before the game Mahorn was presented with his championship ring. He obviously still smarted from his departure, and the ensuing play was physical and emotional. With 10.8 seconds left, the Sixers led, 103-99, and seemed on their way to shutting down Detroit. But from the top of the key, Isiah hit a three-pointer, a bank shot no less. Then came the magic moment. Gminski tried to inbounds the ball for Philly, but Edwards was in his face.

Desperate, the Sixers center threw the ball to Hersey Hawkins, but Isiah broke in front, stole the pass, drove into the lane and fed Dumars for a layup and the lead, 104-103. With 2.5 seconds left, the Sixers went for the win. But Rodman was called for a blocking foul on Barkley. Sir Charles

They beat Houston in overtime to keep their streak alive.

made only one of his two free throws, and the game went to overtime, where Edwards and Dumars, who scored 34, secured the win, 115-112.

"This was our Christmas present to them," remarked an unhappy Barkley afterward. "We'll see them again."

The evening provided just another example of how Detroit had come to rely on Joe offensively. No longer did the writers refer to him as a defensive specialist. Opposing coaches began noticing that Daly was using Dumars to control the clock on offense. "I'm getting to do a lot more now," Joe said. "That's a part of our offense now. Let me clear out and see what I can get, see if I can break the

defense down and get to the rim or pass it off."

As a team, the Pistons were as happy as they had been all season.'

"We could've just thrown the ball up in the air and given up," Dumars said. "But we didn't do that. We have learned that you don't give up."

It was a lesson that would serve them well as the season wore on.

They stamped out wins with a machinelike precision after that. Indiana. Sacramento. New Jersey. Charlotte.

They happened in Charlotte just one night before the Lakers were scheduled to appear. Magic arrived in town with the Pistons on his mind. Detroit and Los Angeles were neck

Mahorn and the Sixers couldn't quite tiptoe away with a March win in the Palace.

and neck in the standings. "Repeating is very difficult," he said when asked about Detroit. "It's not easy, and it won't be easy for them. Of course, they're feeling the pressure. Got to be. Every night."

The pressure was there, but the Pistons seemed to be thriving on it. "We've got a lot to play for, so it's an exciting time of year for us," Isiah said. "The last 21 or 22 games we've been pushing pretty hard. Doing what we're doing takes a toll on your body and your mind. But we're capable of pushing hard and knowing what to do and when to do it."

Isiah had 18 assists as they beat San Antonio in the Palace March 15 to move ahead of the Lakers with the

Quite often, their defense awakened in the fourth period, and they would come from behind to snuff the life out of a close game.

best record in the league, 48-15.

"We want that best record," Dumars declared.

They played like it, particularly defensively. Every game, their team defense seemed to galvanize into an overwhelming display of power. On

these occasions, they would sense their defensive power growing and would hustle to apply it in killer jolts. Every time, this power seemed to snap their opponents. Quite often, their defense awakened in the fourth period, and they would come from behind to snuff the life out of a close game.

They were like a fighter, Isiah explained. "When your opponent lets up, you knock the crap out of him."

"It just happens," Laimbeer said confidently. "The defense is a constant."

The night after beating San Antonio, they won by 25 in Chicago. Then on the 18th, they entertained Dallas and won their 50th game, 104-

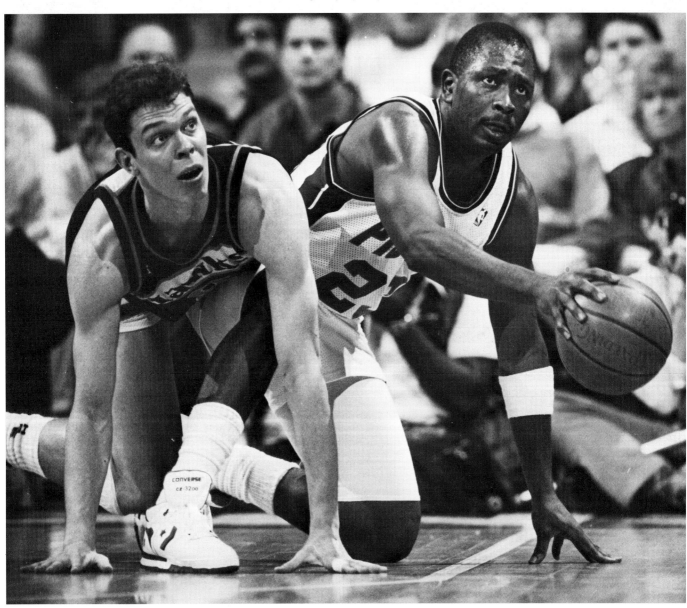

Aguirre played like a new person.

Laimbeer began drawing defensive respect.

The Sixers and Pistons battled in April.

Dumars nursed a broken hand in March.

84, pushing their lead over the Lakers to 1 1/2 games. The beat writers began asking the Pistons if they believed they were invincible. Most of them steered clear of this remark. But a few conceded that, yes, the feeling had crossed their minds.

"Never. Never. Never," Daly said when asked. "I know what can happen in this business. Usually your fall is a mental thing. But we have been tending to business from one to 12, and the guys know where they have been and where they are headed."

They won by 21 in Milwaukee on March 20 to move their streak to 12 straight, 25-1 over eight weeks, 33-4 since January 1.

Even as they won, their minds were on the next road trip, down to Texas. "Those are tough Texas teams," Buddha said. "They're waiting on us down there."

"We realize what's ahead of us," Joe said confidently.

But did they?

DEEP IN THE HEART OF TEXAS

Texas is usually sweet in the spring. But the Pistons arrived there to find a foul, gray, Michigan-like cloud had settled over the plain. The air was cold and wet.

Much worse, their good fortune departed abruptly upon their arrival. They hit the wall March 21 with a loss in Houston that ended their streak. In a way the Pistons seemed almost relieved. They had made their statement. "To have a streak like that today, with all the great scorers in the game, is a tremendous achievement," Houston coach Don Chaney said afterward. "They convinced everybody that a team doesn't need a big man in the middle to win if they're committed to playing team ball and working hard on defense."

That sounded fine, Dumars said, "but the streak will be insignificant if we don't wind up as champions."

Vinnie speculated that they would

get right back on track. But two nights later they encountered a San Antonio team eager to match their intensity. The game reeked of playoffs. The Spurs were in the thick of the Western race and played physically throughout. As usual, the Pistons held nothing in reserve. Even Aguirre had found a knack for defensive fierceness. At one point, Spurs rookie center David Robinson moved into the lane for a jam, but Aguirre took him down. Immediately afterward, he looked over to the bench, where Daly nodded his approval.

The night was filled with such confrontations. As a result, their meeting resembled more a collision than a basketball game. Isiah was battered and afterward showed a deep red gouge in his hip. The game rolled frenetically down the stretch, and the Spurs gave them their second straight defeat, 105-98.

But the loss was bigger than a single game. Dumars had broken his left hand. Over the next few days, there were reports that he might be lost for the remainder of the regular season.

Two nights later, the Pistons lost again, in Dallas, where the crowd booed Aguirre lustily. He seemed taken aback by the nasty reception. Afterward, he admitted to the Dallas media that it hurt. After all, he said, he had left a lot of blood and sweat on the Reunion Arena floor over the years.

Still, he could only be so hurt. It seemed that after a year of practice, Aguirre was finally becoming a real Piston, as Bill Laimbeer defined a Piston. He seemed to be willfully sublimating his ego for the good of the team. Isiah, who had been through the process, watched Aguirre struggle with it.

"It's a tough process," Isiah said. "You have to sit down and have discussions about it with your teammates. It's not something easy to do. But the bottom line—when the question is asked—is, do you want to win? Or do you want to look good? When you put it in that simplicity, most of the guys always choose the right answer. And the people who don't end up leaving."

That threat was always real for Aguirre. He said that he had matured since coming to Detroit, but that he still had to tell himself not to get angry when he didn't get the shots or the playing time he felt he deserved. Sublimating his ego got tougher every time he read about this player or that player getting a fat contract.

"We'll never get to see all the things that I can possibly do with a basketball on this team," Aguirre said. "I understand that.

"I still work on them and do them in practice, but I understand that because of the way we play I probably won't be doing them in a game."

Anyway, the Pistons had larger concerns as March closed like a kitten. Their magic spell had been broken, and suddenly they seemed very vulnerable. Daly, though, was philosophical. For weeks now, he had seen incredible play from his roster. Night after night, they had put forth

Charles lost his shirt but won the brawl in the Palace.

the maximum effort. In the process, they had established something. A new identity based on incredible defense. He loved it.

For a time during the win streak, Detroit had owned the best record in the league. But these setbacks stalled them. And the Lakers eventually passed them on their way to a league-best 63-19 finish. To replace Kareem at center, Los Angeles used a combination of Mychal Thompson and rookie Vlade Divac of Yugoslavia, and it had worked well. As the season closed, the Lakers seemed assured of another trip to the Finals.

And Detroit seemed in real peril. They returned home to beat Charlotte, then paid a trip to Boston Garden to collect yet another loss, 123-111, to finish March at 11-4. Slowly, they began to realize that

they weren't going to catch Los Angeles. Dumars returned early from his injury, but the Pistons put forth an average showing in April to finish 59-23. Although their record was still enough to give them top billing in the Eastern Conference, some observers thought their lukewarm spring was a sure sign that they didn't have the drive to repeat. In 1989, they had focused their entire mindset on claiming the home-court advantage in the playoffs. Mid way through the 1990 season, Isiah had foreseen that the Pistons probably wouldn't have the home-court advantage against the Lakers. Instead, they would have to rely on their ability to win on the road.

"We're smart enough as a team to understand what we have to do," Isiah said confidently.

But Jack McCloskey was worried

Chuck waves off another call.

The Indiana series rekindled their emotions.

The Laimbeer look.

Daly tried to mask his pleasure in concern, but even he couldn't help himself. "We responded like we were let out of a cage," he told the writers.

that his team simply didn't have what it needed. The Pistons had gone 7-4 to close the season and seemed out of sync. Even worse, they had been intimidated in a late-season loss to Mahorn and the Sixers at the Palace. The game featured an ugly brawl and provided Philadelphia the win it needed to clinch the Atlantic Division championship. The primary participants in the fight—Laimbeer and Barkley—were fined $20,000 a piece and suspended for a game. Then for the first time in history, the league fined each team $50,000 for not having better control over their players.

GETTING BACK

The brawl only deepened McCloskey's doubts as the playoffs began. After all, the factors against the Pistons were stacking up. Edwards was hampered by tendinitis in his knee, and the offense was the worse for it.

And there were plenty of distractions. The worst was the persistent report that Daly would be leaving the team regardless of what happened in the playoffs. Soon to be 60, he had been projected as a broadcaster for NBC when the network took over NBA coverage

from CBS for the 1990-91 season. He denied that he had made up his mind, but at the same time he admitted that the year hadn't been easy.

Their first-round opponent was the Indiana Pacers, coached by former Piston assistant Dick Versace. A young, enthusiastic team, the Pacers playbook remarkably resembled Detroit's. And Versace had built their confidence, although forward Chuck Person already had plenty. Before the series started, Person forecast that Indiana would take Detroit in five games.

The Pistons simply smiled.

Indiana fell 104-92 in Game One in the Palace, as Salley returned to his characteristic playoff form with 20 points and 11 rebounds off the bench. "He's like Dr. Jekyll and Mr. Hyde," Buddha said of Salley. "He's a different person during the playoffs, and I'm glad."

So was Jack McCloskey. The Pistons' intensity soon drove his doubts away.

Indiana came back with a fire in Game Two and outrebounded Detroit, 34-32. But it made little difference in the final margin. The Pistons claimed their second playoff win, 100-87.

The series then moved to Market Square Arena in Indianapolis, where the Pacers brought out more fire. They again worked the boards and took a 17-10 lead. The Pistons, however, merely waited for the defensive spell to fall over them.

"We knew exactly what was going to happen out there," Laimbeer explained afterward. "We knew they'd be jacked up, and they'd come out and play emotionally in the first quarter. We talked about it before the

53

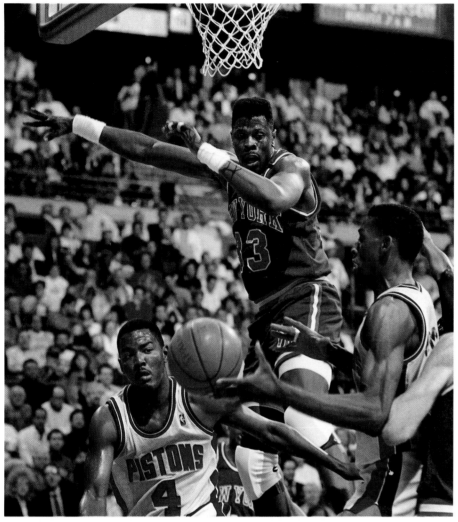

The Pistons subdued Ewing.

game. We said, 'Fine. Let 'em get their little lead. Let 'em have their fun. Then we just keep on going and take over for the rest of the game.' "

The Pistons worked true to that form and turned in another blueprint victory, 108-96, to sweep the series. Over the three games, six players— Isiah, Joe, Vinnie, Laimbeer, Salley and Buddha—had averaged in double figures. And Laimbeer had averaged 14.7 rebounds.

On defense, they held the Pacers to 91.7 points per game.

"I don't envy any team going up against them," Indiana's Reggie Miller said. "They don't give up anything easy."

Their second-round foe appeared to be Boston. But after taking a two-game lead on the Knicks, the Celtics had folded rather strangely, a development that led to the firing of coach Jimmy Rodgers.

Having earned an emotional comeback win, Patrick Ewing and the Knicks came to town to be the Bad Boys' next feast.

Before the series started, Rodman was named the league's Defensive Player of the Year, a development that left him weeping in the press conference announcing his selection. "I went numb when I heard," Rodman told the gathering before breaking down.

He had received 49 of a possible 92 votes for the award. Akeem Olajuwon finished second with 35 votes.

"This award means so much to me," Rodman said. "It means that I'm willing to give up my body and my stats for the good fo the team. And it's great to have the writers recognize that this year. I believe I should have got it last year [when Utah's Mark Eaton was selected]. I

cried when I didn't. But I'm thankful to all the people who voted for me. It means everything to me."

McCloskey helped the sobbing Rodman away from the microphone and later remarked that it was great that a player was emotional enough about the award to cry.

"Dennis is the best defensive player I've ever seen," McCloskey said.

The Pistons, meanwhile, had six days off waiting for Boston and New York to settle up. Thinking the Celtics would win, the Bad Boys had spent their time studying Boston's playbook.

Not to worry, assistant Brendan Suhr said when he learned that the Knicks had won that Sunday April 6. We'll just change books and do a quick study.

Their effort has to go down as one of the best short courses in NBA history. The Knicks appeared rather weary when the series opened three nights later in the Palace. Dumars and Rodman charged up the defense early, while Isiah hit seven of his nine first-half shots. Buddha outhustled Knicks center Patrick Ewing and scored 18 points.

The result was one of the biggest blowouts in NBA history, 112-77. With the score at 102-61, Daly sent in little-used Scott Hastings. "I'm a lot like Red Auerbach's cigar," Hastings quipped. "When I go in the game, it means it's over."

Daly tried to mask his pleasure in concern, but even he couldn't help himself. "We responded like we were let out of a cage," he said.

The Knicks vowed to come back strong in Game Two, and they did manage to tighten the score quite a bit. But the outcome was the same. The Knicks had tied it at 92 with 6:13 left, when Isiah broke loose for three three-pointers. That did the trick. The Pistons took a 2-0 series lead, 104-97.

Besides Isiah's late-game theatrics, Edwards was the charm for Detroit with 32 points on 13 of 19 shots from the floor. Isiah finished 5 of 7 from three-point range. "I've been working on them a lot lately," he said of the bombs. "I felt I could make it."

The Knicks were eager to get back to New York to see if they could salvage things as they had against Boston. Daly was confident, though. "The pressure is on them to take two games in New York," he said.

Ewing, however, gave them reason for pause in Game Three. He scored 45 points with 13 rebounds and led the Knicks to a 111-103 win, pulling the series tighter at 2-1. The Pistons had made only 21 of 35 free throws.

"A blind man could see how we lost," said Rodman, who had been slowed by an upset stomach. "Free throws."

When he finessed a three-point play to give New York a 10-point lead early in the fourth period, Ewing exchanged a high five with filmmaker Spike Lee at courtside. To go with Ewing's offense, the Knicks played inspired defense, allowing the Pistons to shoot just 43 percent from the floor.

But, as Daly had pointed out earlier, the pressure was on them to win two in New York, and they couldn't. Ewing succumbed to foul trouble in Game Four, and the Pistons promptly snatched a 3-1 series lead with a 102-90 win. Ewing's first three fouls had come early, and Knicks coach Stu Jackson was obviously exasperated. "It's very, very difficult for me to coach a game when Patrick Ewing plays only six minutes in the first half," he said.

"You foul, you sit," Laimbeer said flatly.

The New York center came back in the second half to score 30 points, but it was too late. The Knicks pulled close late, but Dumars scored the Pistons' final 13 points to keep the margin.

Rodman's defense played the main role for Detroit, and now the series headed back to Motown. The New Yorkers knew it was over. Vendors in Madison Square Garden were urging fans to buy the last hot dogs of the season as Game Four came to a close. Whether or not they took the dogs, Garden fans did make the most of their opportunity to lambaste Laimbeer. Hastings, who

Michael had to go it alone for much of the Eastern Finals.

had gotten to know Bill since coming to Detroit, continued to be shocked by the enmity opposing fans showed for Laimbeer. So Hastings had T-shirts made up with the slogan "Have You Hugged Bill Laimbeer Today?" and passed them out to the team.

But as always, Laimbeer had his own special salve for the abuse. A playoff win worked wonders for him.

For the first time in the two year history of the Palace, the Pistons had an opportunity to close out a playoff series at home. Usually they wiped out the opposition on the road. The Knicks, at least, were spared that humiliation. New York, in fact, made quite a contest of Game Five. They

took a 23-9 lead at the start, forcing the Pistons to fight back. Detroit edged back in front, 51-49, at the half, but Daly was still fuming. Did they want to go back to New York? he screamed in the locker room.

They answered with a fierce defensive effort in the second half, limiting New York to 35 points, enough for a 95-84 win. "They stifle you," Knicks guard Maurice Cheeks said of the Pistons. "And all the guys they can throw at you. The guys they have coming off the bench aren't just coming in for playing time. They all play significant minutes."

The post-game news got even better for the Pistons. Chicago had eliminated Philadelphia. For the second year in a row, Detroit would have to contend with Michael Jordan in the conference finals, but that was still better than battling the physical Sixers.

Or so they thought.

JORDAN RULED

The relationship between the Chicago Bulls and the Pistons was icy at best, except at the very heart of the competition. When the teams met, the focus of their battle fell on Joe Dumars vs. Michael Jordan. The two men admired and respected each other. Both were conservative, low-key types not given to brashness or bluster. They hadn't known each other personally until a lull at the All-Star game in Miami in February, when Jordan had phoned Dumars' room to invite Joe and his wife, Debbie, up to the Jordans' room for dinner and conversation.

Mike and Joe hit it off quite well.

But when the Eastern Conference finals came around, this new friendship did nothing to dull their competition. In fact, as with the battle between Magic and Isiah, the friendship seemed to goose the competition.

The Pistons supposedly employed the much-ballyhooed "Jordan Rules," a top-secret set of guidelines for countering pro basketball's Air force. Some observers suspected the concept was nothing more than tomfoolery with the media. Whatever. If there really were Jordan rules, they worked just enough to allow the Pistons to escape a seven-game series. What's more, they only worked in Detroit. Which was just fine with the Bad Boys. After all, they held the homecourt advantage.

The premise was pure basketball common sense. Force Jordan to give up the ball. Gang up on him as much as possible. And pray a lot.

A whole lot.

The one problem with this approach was that the Pistons forgot to play offense in Game One. They hit only 33 of 78 from the floor, and one of those was an Isiah Thomas

lob pass to John Salley that inadvertently went in the basket.

As before, Detroit's hell-bent-for-leather defense saved 'em.

"It was more like a rugby match," Chicago coach Phil Jackson said glumly.

Detroit did get 13 rebounds from Worm and eight more from Aguirre. But the key effort was 27 points and plenty of defense from Dumars. "Just give us one hot guy," Laimbeer crowed afterward. "One hot guy. That's all we need."

Dumars was that hot guy. He scored 18 points in the critical third period. And his defense slowed Jordan to 34 points. The rest of the Chicago starters scored a total of 31.

Which was enough for a blueprint Bad Boy ugly win, 86-77.

The other ugly factor was Rodman's ankle, which he sprained late in the first quarter. "I landed wrong on it," he said. "I don't know how. I just hope it doesn't swell up overnight."

Jordan himself got banged up after flying high into the lane in the first quarter. A group of Pistons led by Rodman sort of laid him down on the floor, bruising his hip. "I think I had my legs cut out from under me," Jordan said. "And if so, I don't know who did it. I think it's the type of injury that could linger."

It did linger, at least through the next battle. The Pistons snatched a

The Palace regulars helped stop Mike.

43-26 lead in the middle of the second quarter of Game Two, while Jordan opened stiffly. But then he warmed up a bit and put the Bulls back in front 67-66 at the 8:24 mark of the third.

The Pistons struggled again, making 34 of 73 shots. And again Dumars, who had gotten sick at halftime, was the offensive heat, with 31 points on 12 of 19 from the floor. That propelled Detroit along to a 2-0 lead with a 102-93 win. Meanwhile, Jordan made just 5 of 16 shots to finish with 20 points. Immediately afterward, the Chicago star ripped into the Bulls for their uninspired performance and left the locker room without speaking to reporters. He would later point out that this criticism was directed at himself as much as his teammates.

Moments later, the writers gathered around Joe in the Detroit locker room and asked how he had stopped Jordan.

Dumars looked to the ceiling for help. You don't stop Jordan, he explained.

Game Three in Chicago Stadium proved just how right he was.

Jordan scored 47 and got enough help from his teammates for a 107-102 Bulls win. Isiah had broken out of a 5-for 21 shooting slump to score 36 while Aguirre had 22 points and seven rebounds. But the Bulls won the rebounding battle, 46-36, and the second shots gave them the edge.

"We played stupidly," said Laimbeer, who was 0-for-6 from the field. "Not giving up second shots is one of our strengths. We just did not work hard enough and did not concentrate hard enough."

Ditto that for Game Four, which Chicago claimed 108-101 to even the series at 2-all. On a bad ankle, Rodman had 20 points and 20 rebounds. But it was all for naught. Jordan again had a big night, 42 points, and Chicago's other four starters finished in double figures.

At one point, the Bulls held a 19-point lead, but Dumars scored 24 points and again led the Piston charge. Twice the lead was cut to three, but the Bulls made 18 of 22

free throws to maintain their edge.

Once again, the Pistons had been puny on offense, hitting only 29 of 78 attempts for 37.2 percent. They outrebounded the Bulls 52 to 37 but that didn't help since they couldn't hit the shots. A fan held up a two-sided sign near the Detroit bench. "Something stinks around here," read one side. "It must be Laimbeerger cheese," read the other.

There was some accuracy to the fun. Laimbeer had gone just 1-for-7 from the field. Over the four games of the series, he was shooting just 28 percent.

Daly was sick to his stomach. "I'm fed up with the way our intensity has been," he said. "You can't expect to

just waltz in and repeat as NBA champions. We've had it easy all year. This is the first time in the playoffs that our backs are against the wall, and if we don't respond right now offensively and defensively, we can forget about repeating."

Suddenly the Bad Boys, who liked to keep the pressure on the opponent, found themselves going home and facing a must-win situation.

Fortunately, Edwards and Laimbeer heeded Daly's warnings for Game Five and shook off their slumps. Bill scored 16, Buddha 13, and Aguirre 19 as the Pistons took a 3-2 series lead with a 97-83 win.

Aguirre, in particular, had been vital for the Pistons, with 13 points in

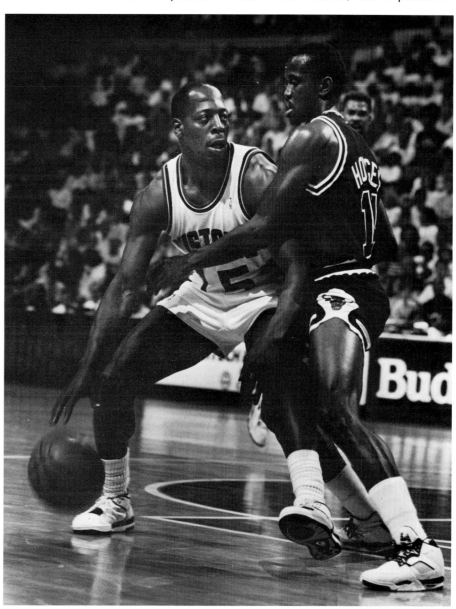

Vinnie had his problems against the Bulls.

Salley was great in Game Seven.

The battle Royal.

Joe to the hole.

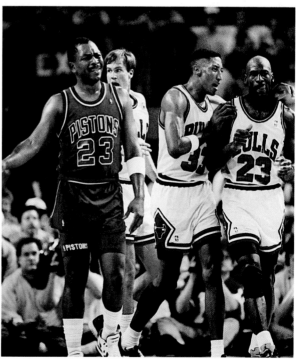

The Game Six loss.

Buck and Zeke both wanted the ball.

the first seven minutes of the fourth period. He had played just nine minutes in the previous game. "I think I can do damage against the Chicago Bulls if I get a chance," Aguirre said, quickly adding that Daly was the coach and he would abide by his decisions.

The other part of the victory equation was again Dumars, who held Jordan to 22 points. Sick again with fever and a cold, Dumars played 38 minutes. The Pistons' other defensive stopper, Rodman, spent most of the night on the bench with his badly sprained ankle. The doctors said there appeared to be bone chips in it from an old injury.

"With Jordan, there's nothing you can do but work, hope and pray, and Joe did all three," Daly said.

Who could have suspected that

they would return to Chicago, hold Jordan to 29 points and still lose in a blowout?

Terrible shooting was again the culprit. The Pistons made just 25 percent of their shots in the third period and watched the Bulls puff a three-point edge into an 80-63 lead to open the fourth.

It got worse. Detroit lost 109-91.

And like that, the Bulls had forced a seventh game, which brought to mind two immediate thoughts:

1) The Pistons had never won the seventh game of a playoff series, and

2) With Michael Jordan, anything could happen in a single game.

"We are more driven than ever to win this thing," Jordan said afterward.

After playing horribly, Isiah

Just as the Pistons were finding new life, the Lakers succumbed suddenly in the Western playoffs.

Thomas had spent the entire fourth period on the bench listening to the gloating of the Stadium crowd. He stewed in the derision.

And there was injury to add to the insult. At Chicago's Midway Airport, a tanker truck backed into the Pistons plane, Roundball One, causing $25,000 damage and forcing the Bad Boys into the delay of a charter home.

Laimbeer flops and then lounges.

Elated with Zeke's late-game theatrics, Worm gives Thomas a boost.

Zeke challenged Porter at every turn.

Somehow, it ended up being a good thing. "We got stuck at the Chicago airport when our plane was damaged," Salley explained to Free Press columnist Mitch Albom. "We had to hang around in this lounge for an hour or so waiting. It's longer than we usually stay together after a game. We started talking, you know, about where we were and what we had to do."

For Laimbeer, the direction was quite simple.

"At some point," he said, "we knew we would be in a seventh game. That time is upon us."

The Pistons got directly to the matter on June 3. With Salley and Aguirre leading a maddening charge, they hammered the Bulls in the second quarter. They shot 82 percent from the field and held Chicago to 20 percent. And they did it by playing like kids. Blocking shots. Swinging fists in the air. Running. Jumping. Shouting. Laughing. Aguirre was the biggest kid of all. He finished with 15 points, while Salley scored 14 with five blocks.

Isiah directed the offense with 11 assists, 21 points and eight rebounds. All together, it combined for a 93-74 Detroit win, giving the Pistons their third straight trip to the Finals.

"It feels good," Thomas said with a big smile.

As usual, it was their defensive invincibility that did the trick.

"We hit a stretch there, and it became almost impossible to score on us," Isiah said. "It was beautiful. It was like we were on a rubber band—everybody was moving in tandem."

THE DALY DOUBLE

Just as the Pistons were finding new life, the Lakers succumbed suddenly in the Western playoffs. They beat Houston in the first round but then strangely came apart in the second round against a young and inspired Phoenix team. The Suns

Another unforeseen factor would be Magic's little buddy, Isiah. He was about to turn in one of the most overwhelming performances in the history of the championship series.

won, 4-1, and in the aftermath Pat Riley decided to leave coaching to become a broadcaster for NBC. Just like that, the team of the '80s had come unraveled.

The Lakers' demise opened the way for the Portland Trail Blazers in the Western Conference. The Blazers had always been considered a talented, dangerous team in the West. But for four straight years they had lost in the first round of the playoffs, and the subsequent frustrations led to team conflicts, particularly between Coach Mike Schuler and 6'7" guard Clyde Drexler. In the middle of the 1988-89 season, the team released Schuler and hired his assistant, Rick Adelman, himself a former Portland guard.

The turnover didn't change things immediately, though. The Blazers still lost to the Lakers in the first round of the '89 playoffs. But in the offseason, they acquired veteran power forward Buck Williams from the New Jersey Nets. Drexler was so impressed by this acquisition that he flew to New York to have dinner with Williams right after the trade.

"I think we have a championship-caliber team, and we're going to get there," Drexler told Williams.

Having spent the first eight years of his career in New Jersey, Williams was more than a bit skeptical of any talk about a championship. But he hadn't been in Portland too long before he, too, realized the potential was there. They had depth at every position. Drexler, the high-flying scoring guard, led them with a 24.3 scoring average, while Terry Porter, a 6-3, 190-pounder, gave them a big

Zeke found the Zone in Game One.

point guard with quickness. Jerome Kersey was a 6'7" leaper at small forward who averaged 16 points a game and an inspired defensive effort just about every night. At center, 7-foot, 270-pound Kevin Duckworth was the ultimate wide body, but one with a deft shooting touch.

"He's a massive human being," Dumars said of Duckworth.

"I'll bet he weighs over 300 pounds," Rodman said.

"He's got the biggest rear end on Earth," Salley offered.

Behind Williams at power forward,

Adelman had options of 6'9", 245-pound Mark Bryant or 6'10" Cliff Robinson. Danny Young and Yugoslavian rookie Drazen Petrovic were the backcourt subs. Veteran Wayne Cooper worked behind Duckworth in the post.

In some respects, they resembled the Pistons, with their depth and belief in fundamentals. "Our guys really believe that when times get tough, if they rebound and defend, they'll win," Adelman said during the playoffs. In fact, they fancied themselves the "Pistons of the West,"

The Pistons grabbed for greatness.

but the two clubs really weren't all that similar. The Blazers were aggressive defensively, but they pressed and went for the steal and liked to use their defense to drive their running offense. They frequently scored off of turnovers.

And while the Blazers were physical, they weren't as stifling as the Pistons. Portland gave up 107.9 points per game, which wouldn't have been acceptable in Detroit. On the other hand, the Blazers' rammin', jammin' offense averaged 114.2 points per season, which revealed a tempo that the Pistons would never want to match. The Blazers ran up big scores despite a .473 team shooting percentage (18th in the league). They were able to do this because Williams, a veteran strong on leadership, infused the entire roster with a rebounding fury.

They finished the regular season at 59-23, then fended off Dallas, San

Antonio and Phoenix in the playoffs to make their first trip to the Finals in 13 seasons. The success brought a return of the "Rip City" mania that had gripped Portland when the Blazers won the '77 championship with Bill Walton. Even through their playoff frustrations of the previous four years, their fans had followed the Blazers, giving the team 569 consecutive sellouts in Memorial Coliseum, the longest such streak in pro sports. Having recently expanded to 12,884 seats, the compact Coliseum created a dread in visiting teams. The Pistons, in particular, didn't like the place. They hadn't won in Portland since 1974.

Once the Lakers had been ousted, most observers began penciling in the Pistons as champions. Even so, the Bad Boys weren't about to get overconfident. They were banged up and sluggish. Rodman's left ankle still hobbled him, and Dumars was slowed

by a pulled groin muscle. For Vinnie Johnson, the ailments were mental. He was in a mild shooting slump.

"Portland is going to be very tough," Isiah said as the Finals opened. "The matchups are what makes this series so interesting. It'll be me and Terry Porter, and that's a draw. It'll be Dumars and Clyde, which is a lot like Joe going against Jordan. It'll be Rodman on Kersey, Buck on Edwards and Bill and Duckworth. Interesting matchups."

But Magic Johnson, who had followed the Pistons through much of the playoffs, looked beyond those obvious pairings. Portland's bench wouldn't be able to match Detroit's, he said. "When Salley, Mark and Vinnie are out there, that's Detroit's best lineup. I think that's where the Pistons get the edge."

Another unforeseen factor would be Magic's little buddy, Isiah. He was about to turn in one of the most

When Isiah wasn't bombing, he slipped inside.

overwhelming performances in the history of the championship series.

Once considered a superstar, Isiah's reputation had dipped despite Detroit's success. For his third, fourth and fifth seasons in the league, he had been paired with Magic on the All-NBA first team. But Thomas fell to honorable mention status during the three seasons, 1988-90, when he led the Pistons to the Finals. The reason? He had sacrificed his personal statistics to make the team better. His scoring average and assists had been fat when he was Detroit's one-man offense. When writers asked why his statistics seemed to have lost their sparkle, Isiah explained that he had placed a priority on winning, not his personal stats. That sounded reasonable enough, but when it came time to vote for the All-NBA teams, their votes went to the big scorers. Thomas understood this reasoning, but he still didn't like it.

Rather than worry about honors and awards, he focused his energy on improving. Bird and Magic had always done something during the summer to boost their games for the upcoming year, so at the end of the '89 season, Isiah decided he wanted to add something to his game. He wasn't a big man, so he couldn't develop a junior skyhook or some power move. Instead, he focused on the three-point shot, spending hours each night in the gym at his home shooting hundreds of jumpers. Often, his shooting sessions would run well past midnight.

When the opportunity for another championship came, Isiah wanted to be ready.

That opportunity arrived with Game One in the Palace on June 5. The Pistons, though, were anything but ready. For 41 minutes, the Blazers used their intensity to control the tempo. They rebounded. They played defense. They scored on offensive rebounds. All of which allowed them to keep the lead. Whenever the Pistons made a run, Portland found an answer. As the game went on, Detroit's difficulties

The Pistons showed their strength.

deepened. With seven minutes left, the Blazers led, 90-80.

Then, during a timeout, Isiah broke an ammonia capsule and whiffed it. "I had seen Larry Bird do it a couple of years ago," he explained later, adding that he hadn't done it very often. "It comes in handy. . . Sometimes you just need something to break up the cobwebs in your head."

What followed was an amazing turn of events.

The Pistons turned up their defense, and it worked. Strong and confident throughout the early going, Drexler and Porter abruptly began making mistakes. They took bad shots and committed turnovers and fouls.

At the same time, Isiah got the Pistons going with a layup and a jumper. Then Dumars completed a three-point play, and Aguirre scored on an offensive rebound. In less than

three minutes, Detroit had tightened the game to 92-89.

Williams gave Portland a little room with a jumper to move it to 94-89, but Isiah reeled off seven straight points. At the 4:18 mark, he stripped Porter of the ball. Adelman wanted a foul on Isiah, but instead, Porter tried to steal the ball back and drew a whistle. Thomas made both free throws, then hit another three-pointer moments later to tie the game at 94.

On Portland's possession, Drexler was whistled for an offensive foul, another call that left Adelman complaining. It was the Blazers' sixth turnover of the period. Thomas exploited it with an 18-footer that gave Detroit the lead, 96-94. The Pistons then got another stop on defense and began searching for a way to expand their lead. Thomas worked the ball just beyond the three-point line, and Porter lay back,

waiting for him to make his move.

At 1:49, Isiah stunned the packed house and a nationwide television audience by sticking the open three-pointer for a 99-94 lead. "He was just tremendous," Adelman said later. "He made all the plays. That three-point shot he made was just a huge play. He wanted the ball. He wanted to take control. And he did it."

"It just kind of happened," Thomas said. "This was a battle of wills, not a battle of skills."

Both teams missed four free throws apiece in the final 90 seconds, but Isiah's outburst made the difference. The Pistons escaped, 105-99.

"We were dead in the water—belly up," Chuck Daly said. "It was just a special player making great shots."

Thomas finished with 33 points, including 10 in a row at crunch time that propelled the Pistons to a 23-4 run. They had won despite shooting 37.4 percent from the floor. The big reason, besides Thomas, was their 19 offensive rebounds, eight of which belonged to Salley.

Both teams got balanced scoring from their starters. Dumars had 20. Laimbeer had 11 with 15 rebounds. But as Magic had projected, Detroit's bench was the other big difference. Led by Aguirre's 18 points, the Piston subs outscored Portland's, 26-7.

The win was nice, but the Pistons wouldn't be that lucky again, Daly said. "We've got to find our offense."

The Blazers were more concerned about stopping Thomas. "We're going to throw a blanket over him, tackle him and pull him over to the sideline," Drexler quipped.

That seemed to be a fitting strategy for Game Two. Whatever the Blazers did, it kept them close enough to win it in the end. Detroit came out strong and took a 31-19 lead, but then the Pistons fell into a rash of turnovers, committing 13 for the half. That was enough to open the way for the Blazers, who charged back to take a 53-48 lead at intermission.

The Pistons made a strong rush in the third, but by then their problem was excessive fouling. Their hacking

Vinnie ended his slump in high style.

and aggressive defense sent the Blazers to the line for 41 attempts. They made 31 of them.

The game tightened in the fourth, and it seemed the Pistons were on the verge of another outburst, this time from Laimbeer. He had scored but seven points over the first three periods, then went wild in the fourth, hitting 19 points over the last 17 minutes. For the game, he laced in six three-pointers, tying a Finals record set by Michael Cooper in 1987.

It was a Laimbeer trey at the 2:59 mark that gave Detroit an 89-86 lead.

But Drexler, on his way to a 33-point evening, quickly answered that with a trey of his own to tie it. The two teams grappled from there until 49.3 seconds were left when Salley soared

The Pistons were upset but not entirely surprised by their blunder. Suddenly, they faced the task of winning in rainy Portland.

Duckworth's mass was much.

to score on a tip-in and drew Duckworth's sixth foul. Salley missed the free throw, but his acrobatics gave Detroit a 94-91 edge.

Five seconds later, Drexler made a free throw. Then at 23 seconds, Isiah proved his mortality by missing a layup. At 10 seconds, Porter tied the game at 94 with a pair of free throws, and it went to overtime when Isiah missed an 18-footer at the buzzer.

The Pistons again surged in the extra period, first on a hook from Edwards, then on a pair of treys from Laimbeer, the second of which gave Detroit a 102-98 lead with 1:30 left. Porter hit another set of freebies to trim the lead to two, then Drexler tied it at the one-minute mark with a 17-footer.

Portland finally took the lead at 104-102, and the Pistons faced a final possession without Isiah, who had fouled out with 1:10 left in overtime.

Chuck was rumored to be leaving.

But Laimbeer promptly bailed them out at 4.1 seconds by hitting a 25-footer for a 105-104 margin. Aguirre came rushing across the court to embrace Laimbeer, who shooed him away.

"After I hit the shot, I looked at the clock and saw there were four seconds," Laimbeer said later. "And in the NBA, four seconds is an eternity."

If not an eternity, it was at least time to work the offense. Portland got the ball to Drexler, and Rodman, who was playing on his bum ankle, promptly hand-checked him. The refs made the call with two seconds left, and Clyde glided both of them for a 106-105 lead.

The Pistons showed that they, too, could set up and shoot on time. Edwards got a good shot from the left of the paint, but rookie Cliff Robinson came over and blocked it at the last second.

Like that, the Blazers had taken away the homecourt advantage. "At times, we played stupidly, unemotionally," said Laimbeer, who finished with 26 points and 11 rebounds.

Porter had 21 points and 10 assists. He made 15 of 15 free throws for the game, setting a new Finals record for the most without a miss.

But it was Drexler's last two that made the difference. "It was a sweet win for us," Clyde said with a grin. "All I wanted to do was make it. Total concentration."

"We had the game under control but we kept sending them to the free throw line," Thomas said, adding that they had wasted Laimbeer's fine effort.

The Pistons were upset but not entirely surprised by their blunder. Suddenly, they faced the task of winning in rainy Portland. "I guess we have to put on our raincoats and win some games there," Laimbeer said.

The Pistons could probably get a win in Portland, most observers suspected. But no one figured they would get three.

From there, the series took an unexpected emotional turn. Dumars' father, Joe Dumars II, died of congestive heart failure an hour and a

Isiah opened up against Portland.

half before the tipoff of Game Three on Sunday. June 10. Mr. Dumars had suffered from a severe diabetes that had forced the amputation of both of his legs in 1985. Joe III, the youngest of seven children, had been very close to his father, who had served with General George Patton in the European Theater in World War II, then had gone on to a 30-year career as a truck driver. To instill the work ethic in his six sons, Mr. Dumars had taken each of them on his grocery truck route. "I was fortunate enough to take all my sons out there with me and teach them how to work," Mr. Dumars said in a 1989 interview. "I think that helped shape their lives. Out of the six, every one of them, they don't mind tackling work."

It was this work ethic that made Joe III so valuable to the Pistons. As his father's condition worsened, Joe realized that the news of his death might come before or during an important game. So Joe asked

Debbie, his wife, not to inform him of any news until after the game had ended. His father had instilled such professionalism in Dumars, and his wife kept his wish.

Daly, his assistants and Isiah Thomas were informed of the news. Joe and the rest of the team weren't told.

It was a crucial afternoon for the Pistons. They had faced a crossroads headed to Portland with the series tied. They had to play without Rodman, whose ankle injury had worsened. He was replaced by Aguirre. The real test came from the venue. In a building where they hadn't won in years, they needed to take at least one of the three games scheduled. True to their style, they wasted little getting the job done. For the first time in the series, Vinnie found his range, making nine of 13 shots for 21 points. But Dumars was the most potent, leading Detroit with 33 points on an array of shots. At one

The Blazer bench just couldn't match Spider and Company.

point in the third period, Portland cut a sizeable Piston lead to 68-60, but Dumars answered with a trey that killed the Blazers' momentum.

"That shot kind of did it," Aguirre said. "They never really got into it again."

Later, Isiah recalled watching Dumars and thinking that moments after he was through, his world would be devastated by word of his father's death. "It was hard to look at him at times," Isiah said.

Moments after Detroit won, 121-106, Debbie Dumars used a courtside phone to inform Joe of his father's death. Shortly thereafter, Dumars left the arena. First reports indicated that he was headed to Louisiana to be with his family. Dumars had spoken with his mother, Ophelia, by phone, and she had informed him that his father's sense of professionalism would direct him to stay on the job and attend the funeral the following Saturday.

Dumars decided he would play but declined press interviews. Faced with demanding schedules and the realities of a business atmosphere, pro basketball players often attempt to draw emotion from any available source. But there was no attempt to exploit this situation for those purposes. Instead, the team seemed to become charged with a quiet determination, adopting an attitude that the job of winning the championship would be completed as swiftly and efficiently as possible.

At first, the Pistons had been elated at taking a 2-1 lead in the series, but the news abruptly subdued them. "Death is strange," said Scott Hastings. "Even if you expect it, it still hits you like a bolt of lightning. But if there's anybody who can handle this, it's Joe Dumars. He's what every father wants their son to be. He's the personification of class and dignity."

Still, there had been much to cheer in their performance. The once-struggling offense had hit better than 53 percent from the floor, and beyond Dumars and Vinnie, the scoring had been balanced, with Aguirre, Edwards and Laimbeer hitting for 11

Joe against Drexler was a great matchup.

points apiece inside. Salley scored another 10 off the bench, and Isiah had yet another strong game, scoring 21 with eight assists and five rebounds.

The Blazers, on the other hand, were infuriated again over the officiating. Williams, Kersey and Duckworth each got into foul trouble in the first quarter. "They take your starting lineup out of the game in the first six minutes—what can you do?" Adelman asked afterward.

Much of the controversy centered on Laimbeer's alleged "flopping" to draw offensive fouls.

"Laimbeer flopped the whole game," Duckworth ragged. "He's done it all along, and they know how he plays. It's a crying shame."

Laimbeer played up the part before Game Three by donning a black hat

he borrowed from Aguirre. Far more than his flopping, his rebounding hurt Portland. He had another 12.

As for the flopping charges, Laimbeer replied, "You gotta do what you gotta do."

Some observers thought the Blazers had become sidetracked and lost their concentration on this issue. Williams, for one, said his teammates should keep their minds on the game. "I'm not going to cry about it," he said. "That's the easy way out."

Rather than worry about fouling, the Blazers desperately needed to play some defense. Giving up 121 points in their first home game wasn't going to win them any championships. Portland had responded to the foul trouble by playing three guards, which forced Daly to go to the three-guard lineup.

Detroit's backcourt took the challenge, outscoring Portland's trio, 76-49.

The Pistons had shot well, Drexler said but added that he didn't think they could keep it up.

The first quarter of Game Four made Drexler's assessment seem sound. The Pistons' shooting percentage dipped below 40 while the Blazers raced off to a 32-22 lead at the end of the period. The outlook worsened for Detroit just minutes into the second quarter when Thomas picked up his third foul. But Vinnie and Dumars took over from there, leading a 9-0 run that pulled the Pistons to 32-31 with 7:49 left in the half. The Blazers tried to answer with ill-timed one-on-one basketball and poor shots. With Dumars running the point and Vinnie blazing away from shooting guard, Detroit kept charging and took a 51-46 lead at intermission.

Portland scored only 14 points in the second period, and things grew worse right after the half. Isiah returned with a fire to score 22 points in the third. His three-pointer at the 2:15 mark pushed the Pistons to an 81-65 lead that quieted the Coliseum. The Blazer fans turned their thoughts to the parking lot, and Detroit seemed to settle in for a comfy ride.

But it was a game of strange twists and turns. Over the next eight minutes, the Blazers suddenly remembered the pressure defense and running game that had gotten them to the championship round. They turned on the gas jets and ran off a 28-11 run of their own. Porter drove for a layup to give them a 93-92 lead with 5:20 left in the game.

In a mere eight minutes, it had gotten interesting again, and was about to get more so.

They exchanged the lead twice until Detroit gained a three-point edge with two minutes to go. The Pistons expanded that to 106-102 on a jumper by Dumars at the 1:16 mark. The Blazers fought back and had a chance to tie it with 35 seconds left, but Buck Williams missed one of two free throws that left them trailing, 106-105.

Four seconds later, in a scramble under the Pistons basket, Laimbeer drew his sixth foul, and Drexler made

The Pistons shut down Portland inside.

both free throws to give Portland the lead, 107-106 with 31.8 seconds left. But that lasted just three-tenths of a second, long enough for Isiah to get off a 22-footer that returned the edge to Detroit, 108-107.

With nine seconds left, Porter attempted to drive on Dumars, but Joe blocked his path. The ball came loose, and Isiah scooped it up and headed the other way. Danny Young quickly fouled him, and an instant later Thomas let fly a 55-footer that went in. The officials quickly ruled it no good, but Thomas made the free throws for a 110-107 lead with 8.4 seconds showing.

Aguirre then fouled Porter at 6.5 seconds, and he made both, drawing

Portland to 110-109. On the ensuing play, Edwards got the ball downcourt to a wide-open Gerald Henderson, who had entered the game seconds earlier.

Henderson took the ball in for what seemed like a harmless breakaway layup. Although he scored to put the Pistons up 112-109, his play gave Portland the ball and 1.8 seconds to get a shot.

The Blazers whipped the ball upcourt to Young, who promptly knocked down a 35-footer from the right sideline. Immediately players from both benches came onto the floor.

Good! Good! the Blazers screamed.

The Pistons played with a quiet determination.

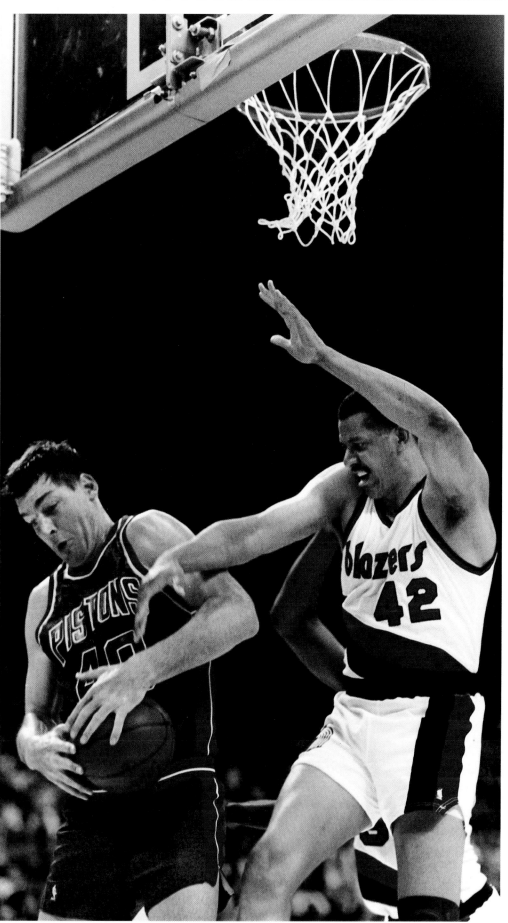

Bill did the board work.

No good! the Pistons answered.

It would be the final game called by 28-year officiating veteran Earl Strom, and it ended in bedlam. Strom huddled the officials amid the din and signalled that the shot was too late. Videotaped replays later confirmed the accuracy of the call, but that didn't stop the Coliseum crowd from screaming for murder.

Actually, both coaches were light in their complaints, the 62-year-old Strom said afterward. "But Chuck Daly did argue one play he was 90 feet from. I told him, 'My eyes are old, but you didn't see it any better.' "

And the Blazers couldn't see it any worse. They were down 3-1. No team in Finals history had ever been that far down and made it back to win the championship.

The Blazers didn't break with that tradition, although for much of Game Five, it appeared they would at least send the series back to Detroit. While the Blazers played like their necks were on the line, the Pistons opened the fifth game slowly, missing seven of their first 11 shots. But they made 15 of their last 19 points of the period, and Detroit held the edge after one, 26-22. The margin was the same at the half, 46-42, but the Blazers shook free in the third period. With 10 minutes to play in the game, they led 77-69.

It was then that Vinnie Johnson went on the first of two scoring binges. He had struggled earlier in the game. But he scored all of Detroit's points in a 9-0 run to give his team a 77-76 edge with 6:35 to go. The Blazers stepped up their pressure and again built a lead. At the 2:05 mark, they pushed it to 90-83, and suddenly observers began turning their thoughts to Game Six in Detroit.

At just that point, Vinnie found his magic again, and the Blazers answered with ineptitude. Johnson scored seven points in Detroit's astounding 9-0 run to close the game and the series, 92-90.

In the final seconds, Isiah worked the ball up top, but he was covered. So he sent the ball to Vinnie, who had Kersey draped all over him. But ball

The Smile said it all.

of muscle that he was, Johnson launched a 15-footer from the right sideline with 0:00.7 seconds on the clock. (His teammates would later take to calling him 007, the James Bond of Basketball). One of his typical low-projectile missles, it just cleared the rim, and punctuated Portland's nightmare with a gentle swish.

The Blazers had lost three straight at home. Bad Medicine.

And because he led the house call, Isiah was named the series MVP. He had scored 33, 23, 21, 32, and 29 points in the five games. From three-point range, he had made 11 of 16 shots. For the series he had averaged 27.6 points, eight assists and 5.2 rebounds, a performance that caused him to unleash his full smile afterward.

"You can say what you want about me," he told the writers, "but you can't say that I'm not a winner."

Vinnie, too, had plenty to smile about. He had scored 16 points, 14 of them under a stinging pressure. One of the few players to average double figures in scoring over his career while never a starter, his performance had finally brought him the spotlight.

"It's something you dream about," he said.

The Finals was something to dream about. But as sweet as this second championship was, it couldn't deliver the Pistons from the hassles of real life, to which they returned after a subdued celebration.

Joe Dumars made his father's funeral on that Saturday, having lived up to the family's tradition of hard work and professionalism.

Vinnie, too, had plenty to smile about. He had scored 16 points on the evening, 14 of them under a stinging pressure.

In the joy of celebration, the city of Detroit found itself faced with a plague of random violence. Eight people died in incidents related to the celebration, a chilling development for the Pistons.

Isiah arrived home to find his own wife crying in front of a television over a news report that his name had surfaced in a gambling investigation. "I don't deserve this," he said and protested his innocence. The authorities involved in the case came to his aid, maintaining that Thomas was in no way a target of their investigation. Instead, he had been a victim of aggressive and sensationalistic reporting. The air was cleared, but the incident dampened his feelings of accomplishment.

For Chuck Daly, the hassles of real life involved the decision he had to make. NBC had just outbid CBS for the rights to broadcast the NBA, and the network wanted Daly as an analyst. He would turn 60 in July, and the pro basketball lifestyle seemed rougher every year. The network offered a pie job with a fat financial package.

Ultimately, though, Daly decided to stay. After all, his team had a chance to win three consecutive league titles. The lure of history was strong for Chuck Daly. But it was much more than history. At its simplest form, it was an opportunity to keep winning. Long before the NBA had ever thought of having a history, the shiny feeling of winning was what had kept everybody going.

Chuck Daly had gotten a good taste of it in his seven seasons with the Pistons.

And he wanted more.

His work done, Joe's thoughts turned to home.

Zeke and Daddy Rich get richer.

The hero gets a hoist.

Zeke Goes Zone

They call it the Zone. It's not an illegal defense, or even the name of a new science-fiction TV series. There's no twilight to it, and no weird plot line.

Still, it is something of a netherworld, where time and space and performance merge magically. It's the Zone, where the shots fall and everything basketball is perfect. Or nearly so.

Every player wants to go there as often as possible. But you can't buy tickets.

Going to the Zone is a special gift, and it just happens.

Which means it is also a paradox. You have to want to go there, but not too badly. You have to be a little bit greedy, but greed won't get you there.

You have to practice hard just to hope you can go. But in the games you can't try too hard to reach the Zone because you usually fail miserably and your team suffers.

In short, the Zone is a wonderful, elusive state of performance. Visitors form an elite club.

Perhaps more than anyone else in the NBA, the Pistons guards have shown a knack for finding the Zone at just the right time in recent seasons. In fact, Vinnie Johnson's nickname "The Microwave" suggests just how quickly he can launch into a scoring spree. Just like a microwave, he seems to jump the bounds of physical possibility. His quick trips to the Zone are almost too numerous to count, except that two come to mind rather easily. On March 1, 1989, he scored 19 straight points against Utah, a Piston club record. But his grandest display of all came last June when he took over the fourth quarter of Game Five of the NBA Finals. First he scored nine straight points to pull

It is something of a netherworld, where time and space and performance merge magically.

Detroit back into a tie with Portland. Then over the last two minutes, he scored the game's final seven points, his last jumper just clearing the rim with :00.7 seconds on the clock to give the Pistons a 92-90 win and their second NBA title.

Of all his hot nights, this was the one to remember, a grinning Vinnie said afterward.

Although his career is young, Joe Dumars, too, has his memories from the Zone. He scored a career-high 42 points with 11 assists and zero turnovers at Cleveland in April 1989, a performance that gave Detroit the Central Division crown. In the third quarter of that game, he scored 24 points, tying a club record.

"Joe was absolutely incredible, on fire," Chuck Daly said afterward.

"I wasn't thinking about anything else other than just getting room to get the shot off," Dumars said. "That's all I needed."

Then, during the 1989 Finals against Los Angeles, Joe again went Zone tripping and emerged with the championship MVP trophy. In the third period of Game Three, he scored 21 points, including 17 straight.

At one point during the outburst, Isiah Thomas looked at Dumars and asked what play he wanted to run.

"Just the ball," Dumars replied. "Just give me the ball."

Once in the Zone, nothing more is needed.

Just the ball.

ZEKE'S TIME

But, of Detroit's three world-class guards, it is Isiah who has enjoyed the truly unique relationship with the Zone. He entered it often enough during his high school and college career. But his first big trip there as a pro came in the 1984 playoffs against New York. In a Game Five showdown with the Knicks, Zeke scored 16 points in 94 seconds of the fourth quarter. It was an incredible outburst that pulled the Pistons out of a deep hole, but it didn't bring Detroit a win.

Three years later, in the 1987 playoffs against Atlanta, he scored 24 points in a quarter.

But it has been during critical junctures of the Finals that Thomas has done his most prominent Zone work.

For example, take Game Six of the 1988 championship series against the Lakers. The Pistons were down, 56-48, early in the second half, when

Thomas scored the next 14 points in trancelike fashion—two free throws after a drive in the lane, then a five-footer off an offensive rebound, followed by four jumpers, a bank shot and a layup.

With a little more than four minutes to go in the period, he landed on Michael Cooper's foot and had to be helped from the floor. Despite a severely sprained ankle, Isiah returned 35 seconds later and continued the offensive assault. By the end of the quarter, he had hit 11 of 13 shots from the floor for 25 points, setting an NBA Finals record for points in a quarter. Better yet, he had driven his team to an 81-79 lead.

The Lakers battled back to stop him, and Thomas finished the game with a jammed left pinkie, poked eye, scratched face, ballooned ankle, 43 points, eight assists, and six steals. Even that wasn't quite enough, though. The Lakers won, 103-102.

"What Isiah Thomas did in the second half was just incredible," Lakers' Coach Pat Riley said afterward.

Magic Johnson was even more impressed: "I think he was just unconscious," Johnson said. "I think he said, 'Okay, I'm going to take this game over.' I've seen him do that before. He was in his rhythm. When he starts skipping and hopping, that means he's in his rhythm. That means he's ready."

By the 1990 Finals, Thomas had dispensed with the skipping and hopping for the most part, but his game remained every bit as Zoneworthy.

The Pistons were trailing Portland by 10 points with about seven minutes to go in the fourth quarter of Game One when Zeke zoomed off to the magic place. He scored 16 of his game-high 33 points to lead the Pistons on a 25-9 run that brought them a 105-99 win.

Then in the critical third quarter of Game Four, he scored 16 straight points in an amazing display of three-point shooting. For the series he would make 11 of 16 treys for an astounding 68 percent.

The feeling afterward was an old

Like Isiah, Mike owns a piece of the zone.

familiar glow for Thomas, almost as if he could travel to never-never land any time he pleased. "It's great," he said of the Zone. "You put in all the hours of work to become that perfect player, and for that five- or six-minute period, you become that player."

The state has often been called "unconscious," but Isiah says there's nothing unconscious about his personal Zone. "You remember it," he said. "You remember every play, every incident."

While it doesn't cause blackouts, the Zone does suspend animation in a sense. "Everything on the court seems to get slower," Isiah says. "Everything slows down for you. Everything you do goes right. Be it rebounds or shots."

And in this slowed state, he moves faster while everybody else seems trapped at another level.

CONTROL

The irony in all of this, of course, is that the Pistons have won two NBA championships by relying on their guards' ability to get Zoned out, but for years Isiah has had to avoid going to the Zone too often.

He came to Detroit in 1981, when the Pistons were mired in misery and he was their great offensive salvation. As a young player, he was more than happy to fit that need. He served up great helpings of flash and dash on offense, scoring at will, reaching for the Zone every night.

For a time, it was fulfilling. But as time wore on, he became impressed by the futility of the situation. It seemed that the more he scored, the less Detroit won. And Zeke hated the losing. The scoring was fun, but what he really wanted to do was win. Besides, he found it boring to come down the floor and have nine other faces staring back at him while he got lost in an offensive trance.

Fortunately, things began changing. The team got more talent, and Chuck Daly became coach. For Isiah, the Zone became a candyland. He had to rein in his sweet tooth. He had to stop looking to go there. Chuck Daly wanted him to change, to become more of a point guard and less of an offensive dominator.

Isiah wanted that change, too, because it meant the chance to win a championship. But there were tough new things to learn. The toughest part of the change would be deciding when to deliver the ball to his teammates and when to call his own number.

For answers to these questions and others, he would make late-night phone calls to his friend Earvin Johnson on the West Coast. Having won a batch of NBA titles, Magic cheerfully offered instruction to his little buddy with the lowly Pistons.

"It's no different than trying to learn algebra or geometry in high school," Isiah said of the lesson he learned about toning down his offensive urges. "The first couple of weeks, you struggle. You struggle bad. Then all of a sudden one day you look on the blackboard, and it registers."

It helped that he had the ultimate teacher.

"I hate that I taught him," Magic would say later. "That's the only thing. I should go back and kick myself."

"Just because the teacher teaches, the onus is always on the student to learn," Isiah said. "If you can't learn from the lessons being taught, you're just not a very smart student."

Isiah learned the lesson quite well. He became so good at sublimating his own ego, at forgetting about his own statistics, that observers in the media, even opposing coaches and players, began thinking he wasn't as good as he once was. That bothered Isiah some, but not too much. After all, once he stopped trying to go to the Zone so much and once Pistons management found the right talent, they started winning championships.

Still, it hasn't been easy for Isiah.

Thomas has no fear.

The lure of automatic scoring is practically addictive. The temptation is always there. In each game, Isiah has to fight the urge to beam himself into the Zone.

"Every night, the guy I'm playing against is always at a disadvantage," he says, "because defensively the point guard position is not as good a defender in terms of size, strength and quickness, as the players at other positions. So every night I have a big advantage."

It takes quite an effort to fight the urge to take over games, he says. "You have to be disciplined enough not to look at it as an individual thing, but as a team thing. It gets tough some nights, really tough, because you know if you come out and do your thing, if you take your guy and get 35 every night, you look good.

"But the rest of the team doesn't develop."

And then, he says, the team will come to those nights when it needs seven or eight people playing well, and only two can play.

Then, he says, he would probably be a big star again in observers' eyes, and the Pistons would be losers.

FRIENDSHIP ON HOLD

Things have changed between Magic and Isiah now.

Student and teacher have become the fiercest of competitiors, which has had its effect on their friendship. No longer does Isiah feel comfortable making his late-night calls for advice and help.

"I think we're both at the level now," he says, "where we're competing and we're chasing the same dream and the same goals. So for one of us to give away secrets would not be a smart thing to do."

There is no need for phone calls

now, Magic says with a laugh. "He's learned all he can learn. They're the champs. He knows what he has to do."

Isiah won't say that the situation has hurt his friendship with Magic, but it has changed it.

"I think it has enhanced our friendship in some ways," he says. "I think we can separate the difference and understand that we compete hard against each other. When you're competing for high stakes, such as we are, sometimes your friendship can't be what you'd like it to be.

"He and I will always be great friends, and when this is all said and done, we'll be able to look back on it.

"But in order to compete at this level, sometimes your friendship has to take a back seat. Our relationship is there, but the friendship is on hold."

There is no question the friendship has changed, Magic says. "It's not the same. Playing against each other twice in the Finals has definitely changed our relationship. All around. It had to. It's not anything bad. It's a thing we both understand. Hey, if we're playing them in the Finals, things have to change. They're slamming us. We're slamming them. Hard fouls. We're each going for the win. We have no time to be friends."

THE ULTIMATE POINT

Isiah took Magic's teachings to heart and became a true point guard, looking to everyone else first, then to himself as the last option.

"My role is different every night because every team we play is different," he says of his responsibility. "Every team has a different weakness that you can attack. Being at the point, I have to be able to read that weakness and exploit it. The exploitation doesn't always have to come from me."

First, he has to find who is hot. If no other Piston is, then he has to try to make something happen.

But that isn't a hard and fast rule. Whatever he does, Isiah is guided by his very special instincts. On his best nights, he senses what will work and goes to it.

In the third quarter of Game 4 in

Vinnie and Isiah smile after their zone tripping in the Finals.

the 1990 Finals, he didn't waste time searching. He had gotten into foul trouble and spent much of the first half on the bench. But when he returned to the game, he pushed himself into the Zone. "I sensed Portland was in trouble emotionally and physically," he explained. "I just wanted to keep some pressure on them, to keep them having to make plays. I got hot and just started shooting the ball well."

More specifically, he made four three-pointers that deflated the Trail Blazers. It was an incredible display of confidence and shooting, but it didn't just happen and it wasn't the result of some magic trance. It was the product of long-range planning.

At the 1989 All Star game in Houston, Isiah decided to develop a consistent three-point shot. After the Pistons won the championship that spring, he renewed his committment to the three-pointer. "I looked back and I said to myself that every year Magic added something good, or Bird added something good to his game," he recalled. "And it was usually an

inside move. Well, I can't add an inside move, so I went out and worked on my three-point shot."

Larry Bird had developed his three-pointer prior to 1986, and it resulted in his most successful season ever. The Boston forward said the ability to score from anywhere on the floor left him feeling unstoppable. Isiah was seeking that same kind of confidence.

So he began practicing at home in his personal gym every night after dinner. He would shoot hundreds of shots. He imagined himself facing every kind of tough defender. He practiced off balance, on balance, from all angles and positions.

"You practice the tough shots because the defenses will be taking certain things away from you," he explains. "You know that you're not gonna be able to get your feet together and get set perfectly to shoot the ball."

So you get ready to face the elements.

Even though he worked that hard, Isiah didn't feel comfortable enough

The friendship with Magic has changed.

with the shot to take it regularly during the 1989-90 season. He wanted to be able to take it without questioning himself. He wanted utter and complete confidence. By the time the playoffs arrived, he had it.

Isiah figures circumstances might force him into taking four to five long shots in the average game. Getting ready for those four to five shots could mean the difference between a win and a loss, between success and failure, between a championship and a summer in hell.

"You may shoot the ball for two hours straight every night in practice, and you may take 700 to 800 shots," he says. "You practice 800 shots to come out and take four or five three-point shots in a game. You practice 200 times a night to make that one big shot in a game.

"You have to put in enough time and enough work so that when that one shot comes, you drill it."

If you don't make the shot, the other team will likely fastbreak the other way and score, he says.

The only way to live with such pressure is to practice.

Every night.

THE REPUTATION

Last spring a general manager in the NBA's Western Conference was discussing the true superstars in today's game. There are only about a half dozen real stars playing in the league, the GM said and then named them.

Isiah wasn't included on the list.

Another Western Conference general manager was asked for his list of true stars. He, too, failed to include Detroit's point guard.

What keeps Isiah out of the top echelon? he was asked.

"He needs a better shooting percentage," the GM replied.

Isiah has heard this comment often during his career, but he doesn't agree with it. He says shooting percentages are misunderstood.

"A lot of my shots come at the end of the shot clock when we've exhausted all possibilities," he says. "You're standing out there with five to six seconds to go and you've got to make something happen. If I take 14 shots a game, five of those shots are in those last-second situations. Chances are you'll make one out of five."

Most observers, he says, fail to recognize that guards work differently from the way forwards and centers do. His critics should check the history books and see how other guards shot, he says. "I do okay when stacked up to some of them."

A quick check shows that two of the great playmakers in NBA history, Jerry West and Oscar Robertson, shot about 47 and 48 percent respecitvely for their careers. Isiah has shot just above 46 percent over his nine years in the league.

But it's not just the percentage of shots you make. It's when you make 'em. Isiah has always shown the ability to answer in the big games.

Will his performance in the 1990 Finals means that he now joins the elite? Should Isiah now be considered a true superstar?

Jack McCloskey thinks so. The Detroit general manager has seen quite a bit of basketball over the years, and seldom has he witnessed a guard taking over a big game the way Isiah did in the 1990 Finals. He saw West and Robertson do it, McCloskey says, but no one else.

Make no mistake about it, Isiah wants to be considered among the best. It's only human. "If it happens, that's a very special honor," he says, "and it's something I would be very gratified to receive."

But if it doesn't, he won't loose any sleep over it, except maybe when he's up late at night shooting.

After all, he says, "when your basketball team has done what our team has done, you're doing all right."

You're going to the Zone just enough.

The cult of the Worm.

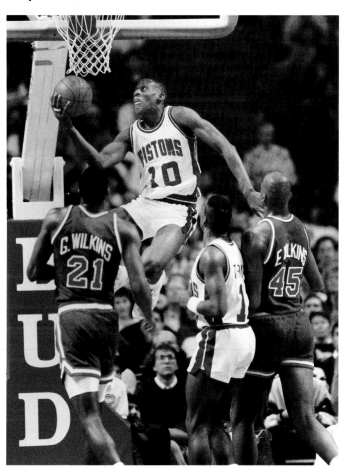

Nureyev of the nets.

Air Worm

He is Air Worm, Detroit's Nureyev of the nets. Dennis Rodman will never be confused with Michael Jordan, but, as evidenced by the accompanying photographs, the Piston forward does possess a uniquely acrobatic style, which he has used to thrill Motown crowds for the past four seasons.

He spins. He flies. He leaps. He dives. He slides. He weeps.

Whatever he does, he never stops. Not even at night.

"I try to sleep," he says, "but basketball just seems to take me over. It just goes and goes. I do something to try to relax, but I can't relax before a game. I'm just so hyper."

The Worm nickname comes from his wiggling while playing pinball as a youngster. "I've got Nintendo now," he says, "so that's taken over. I take it on the road wherever I go." The video games help soak up some of his hyperactivity.

But, for Dennis Rodman, there's nothing like hoops.

Does he slow down even when the season is over? "Somewhat," he says. "Maybe a week or two. But after that, I'm like, I gotta get back to what I was doing."

What he does is create non-stop hassles for the Pistons' opponents.

"I don't think there's ever been anyone like him before," said Chicago coach Phil Jackson, an old NBA hand who played with the New York Knicks championship team of 1970.

When not in the game, Rodman can often be seen on the sideline, running in place. "I'm always like that," he says. "I just like to stay loose."

Some observers have pointed out that Rodman probably wouldn't have made it in the league a few years back. The NBA used to be strictly an offensive game, and Rodman isn't much of a pure shooter or even a scorer.

But now pro basketball has evolved into the age of great defensive players, and the Worm is one of the greatest.

Pistons General Manager Jack McCloskey says Rodman is simply the best defensive player he's ever seen.

The rest of the league seems to agree. In February, his defensive and rebounding skills brought his first selection as an All-Star. Then, in June, he was named the NBA's Defensive Player of the Year for 1989-90. And for the second consecutive year, he was voted to the league's All-Defensive first team (Piston Joe Dumars also was a first-team selection).

"I was extremely happy because the coaches made the

Air Worm.

selection," the Worm said. "That means that coaches recognize that you are working really hard and shutting people down."

Rodman moved into Detroit's starting lineup at mid season last year after spending most of his career coming off the bench. At the time, he was merely replacing an injured Mark Aguirre. But when Aguirre returned, Chuck Daly decided Rodman should remain the starter. The coach figured the team needed Rodman's defense as a starter and Aguirre's offensive boost off the bench.

That approach worked well enough to take the Pistons to their second championship last spring, although it's not entirely clear whether he will continue to start for the 1990-91 season.

Rodman insists that the issue doesn't concern him.

"I don't like starting," he says. "I'm a role player, not an offensive threat. I'm not the main go-to man. I'm the guy who comes in and sparks the team and does things. Shut people down and rebound, things like that."

Daly, too, likes Rodman coming off the bench. After all, the psychological edge is substantial. An opposing team will open a game by making its best run at Detroit. Then Daly shifts gears and inserts Rodman. He comes on to the floor creating mayhem, a loose cannon on the opponent's deck. Like a great ballet artist, he has no fear of the floor. Rodman is quick on the double team and has a swift efficient box-out on the defensive boards.

Not only is his defense good, it is frequently beautiful to watch. Defense isn't supposed to be that way. It's supposed to be an ugly thing, one of the less-savory aspects of the game. But the Worm pirouettes and prances. Pure Nureyev.

To go with his defensive effort, he has phenomenal rebounding ability. "I'm making it an art for me," he says. "I'm not as big as a lot of players, but I'm getting to be smart at getting rebounds."

Why aren't other players around the league able to rebound with him? Rodman is asked often.

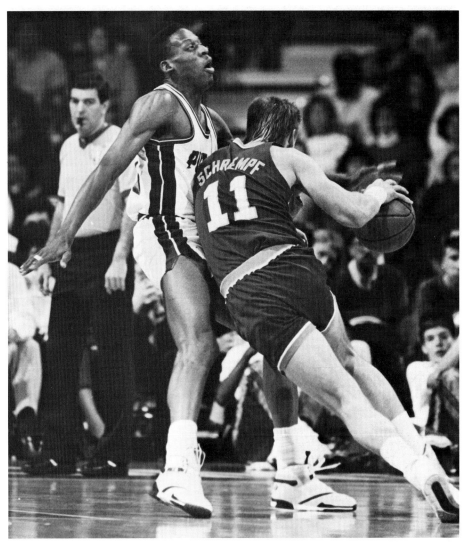

Great defense.

He answers that he simply has a sixth sense for the ball. And his physical gifts help, too.

"I use my leaping ability and quickness to try to tip tip tip the ball and get it," he explains.

Playing Rodman is like playing a rat, Scottie Pippen of the Chicago Bulls said during last year's playoffs. "He's so active, he keeps moving all the time. Even when he doesn't get the rebound, he's keeping the ball alive. You definitely feel it when he's in there. Whenever we prepare for the Pistons one of our main goals is to keep Rodman off the boards. But that's almost impossible to do."

"It's like playing against a guy on a pogo stick," agreed Horace Grant, Pippen's teammate.

Rodman's other great advantage is his natural conditioning. "If you jump jump jump, and you still have

something left at the end of the game, that tells you right there you're in great shape."

He was hampered by a badly sprained left ankle in last year's playoffs.

Even so, he still got 20 rebounds— 10 offensive and 10 defensive— in a game against the Bulls.

If they want to look for a flaw, observers comment that his game is absolutely devoid of offense. That is accurate to some extent, but not nearly as accurate as it used to be. In his fourth season as a pro, Rodman began to develop a turnaround jumper.

The jumper helps, but don't look for Rodman to become a primary option in Detroit's offense. At least not any time soon. The Pistons like his game just the way it is.

Daughter Alexis has a hold on the Worm's heart.

Emotion is a big part of his game.

Rodman rocks with the Hawks.

Hammer time.

Twirl your partner.

The Ringmaster.

The Three-Ring Circus

The Detroit Pistons will make a run at their third straight NBA title in 1990-91. Their traveling review promises a little bit of everything. High-wire walkers. Trapeze artists. Lion tamers. Clowns. Zebras. Racing dots. Assorted animal acts. The proceedings should be fascinating. Mr. P.T. Barnum couldn't put on a better, or Badder, show.

That old ringmaster himself, Chuck Daly, has decided to play the impresario for another season.

And central casting has brought back the major stars (the negotiations for Vinnie Johnson's new contract were ongoing at press time). There's Zeke and Broadway Joe and Worm and Spider and Buddha and Flopper Bill and Mister Mark and Microwave and Fastbreak Hastings and Bedford. To go with them is a pack of rookies and free agents hoping to catch a ride on the band wagon.

Keeping this show on the road seemed to weary the ringmaster last season, so he entertained the idea of leaving Detroit to become a broadcaster for NBC or TNT.

"Insiders" said there were numerous reasons for his leaving. After all, Chuck had won an NBA championship. And he was nearing 60, which meant it was time for him to give up the grind of coaching. Plus it appeared that his relationships with his players were starting to wear thin. This wasn't a knock at Chuck or the Pistons. It was just a fact of life in the league, where most relationships are lucky to last a few seasons. Chuck had worked seven years with Isiah Thomas and had driven his club to three consecutive appearances in the Finals.

That's a lot of driving.

His purported departure worried General Manager Jack McCloskey,

While the rumors of Daly's leaving swirled around Motown, McCloskey remained convinced that Chuck would come back to the show.

but while the rumors of Daly's leaving swirled around Motown, McCloskey remained convinced that Chuck would come back to the show. After all, Daly appeared fatigued, not burned out.

But the rumors persisted. The deal was supposedly as good as done, the insiders said.

Then something dramatic happened. The Pistons won their second consecutive title. Suddenly Chuck Daly had a chance to coach his team to three straight championships. Like that, the alternatives had changed. Instead of leaving the hassles of coaching, he was now walking away from a dream.

How could Chuck Daly work years as a coach, then turn his back on the chance to make history, to win three

straight championships?

The answer was, he couldn't.

He talked with a variety of friends and coaches—Billy Cunningham, John Madden, Al Davis—and asked them how you knew when you were ready to give up coaching. Then he tried to think what it would be like when training camp started in October and he wasn't there. He couldn't bear the thought.

"There was no question," he said. "The lure of coaching was still there."

Actually, it wasn't just the opportunity to win another championship; it was the coaching itself. "When you do it all your life and that's all you know, it's not that easy to walk away," Daly explained. "It's something you know how to do and what to expect. It's comfortable. It's familiar."

Despite the sense of familiarity, Daly will be leading the Pistons into new territory in 1990-91. Their search for a third straight title has given him much reason to think. Every year, it seems, the wire on the Pistons' high-wire act just gets thinner and higher.

"I watched Pat Riley and the Lakers try to do it," Daly said of Los Angeles' attempt to win their third straight in 1989. "They looked like they got tired. We have to be very careful."

HISTORY AND THE FUTURE?

The Boston Celtics won eight straight titles between 1958 and 1966. After his team won their seventh straight in 1965, reporters asked coach Red Auerbach if winning had become old hat. "The thrill never goes from winning," he said. "But maybe the reasons change. First, it was just trying to win a title. Now it is a question of going down as the

Daly makes a point.

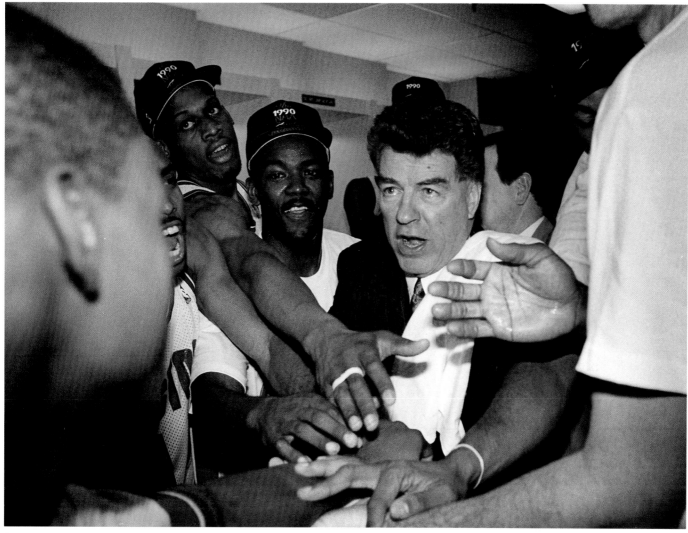

The lure of coaching was strong for Chuck.

greatest team of all time. That stimulates you."

It appears that the Pistons are similarly stimulated. Asked if the chance to make history would help motivate the Pistons, McCloskey said, "I think our guys are very much aware of it."

The question, of course, is just how much history can the Pistons make?

"You'd have to go a long time before you matched the Celtics," McCloskey said.

Bob Cousy, Boston's Hall-of-Fame guard, says that winning championships was tougher way back when because the league's talent was more concentrated in eight to 10 teams.

McCloskey agrees. "It's watered down," he says of the modern NBA. "You got 27 teams instead of eight. If

you cut it down to eight teams today, there are a lot of these guys who are considered stars today who wouldn't even be in the league. The more teams there are, you're gonna have some bad teams, and the teams that are good are just gonna eat them up."

Still, he points out, modern obstacles do bring something of a historical balance. Today's game is affected by agents and television and huge player contracts and salary caps that the old pros didn't have to contend with. All of those things conspire against the team mentality.

Which makes the Pistons all the more special.

"They just worry about victories," McCloskey says proudly. "They're almost totally self-motivated."

Asked what gives the Pistons their special championship chemistry, McCloskey replied, "There's a

misconception that chemistry means everybody gets along, that everybody's a big happy family. I don't think we had that kind of chemistry. Our chemistry evolved around leadership, from Isiah Thomas, Bill Laimbeer, Joe Dumars, Vinnie Johnson in a quiet way, John Salley in a flamboyant way. They're all individuals. That's our chemistry. Our chemistry is not in loving each other. But there's a great deal of respect among the players we have.

"Our guys are close enough. It's not like the Pittsburgh Pirates family with Willie Stargell and all that. We've had guys squabble during the year, and squabble with the coach and a lot of things.

"We don't have anything major. We have the usual little things. Guys want more playing time. Or somebody doesn't get the ball. Or we

Just before camp opened, the Pistons signed free-agent center Tree Rollins, shown here in a tussle with John Salley.

don't execute properly. Little things."

The leadership keeps them from becoming big things, McCloskey says.

Like the Celtics, the Pistons have built their championship success from the basement up. When Auerbach arrived in Boston in 1950, the Celtics had never had a winning season. When McCloskey came to Detroit in December 1979, the Pistons were stumbling their way through a 16-66 season.

It was what McCloskey called "expansion-level" basketball. Four seasons later, Detroit hired Chuck Daly and the team moved above the .500 level for the first time in years. But McCloskey didn't see the early building as the big challenge.

"It's not hard to go from the expansion level up to respectability," he said. "I think it's hard to go from respectability up to the elite class."

It took five seasons, but Daly moved them into championship contention in 1988. The Pistons just

barely missed in 1987, losing a hard-fought Eastern Conference championship to the Celtics in seven games.

Looking back, McCloskey says Detroit could have won four titles between 1987-90. "We should have," he adds. "We had the best team for four straight years."

If you have enough young players you can stay at that elite class for five, six years, McCloskey figures.

Applying his formula, does that mean Detroit has a possibility at two more titles?

"We've got a legitimate shot," he says. "We still have a lot of young good players. And we have two guys—Laimbeer and Edwards—who might have come off the best year they've ever had."

Isiah Thomas says the team has a chance of winning at least two more. But he fears the loss of Rick Mahorn in 1989 means the extra load on Laimbeer and Edwards will wear down the Pistons' frontcourt. The key,

Isiah says, will be for McCloskey to come up with yet another personnel miracle. In other words, find a way to get LSU's Shaquille O'Neal or Georgetown's Alonzo Mourning.

The Pistons, though, haven't been built with that type of dominant player, and McCloskey isn't staking the team's future on any miracles. "Those are the types of players that everybody is seeking," he says. "You get an Alonzo Mourning you have a chance to do something. But our hope is the free-agent market. We're always looking."

The Pistons's strength has been the solid rotation of their first eight players. But, even after having won two championships, McCloskey says he is not afraid to change that rotation.

"We've changed it before," he says. Anyone familiar with the Pistons knows that he is not making an idle boast.

True to his word, McCloskey signed free-agent center Tree

Laimbeer may need help in the frontcourt.

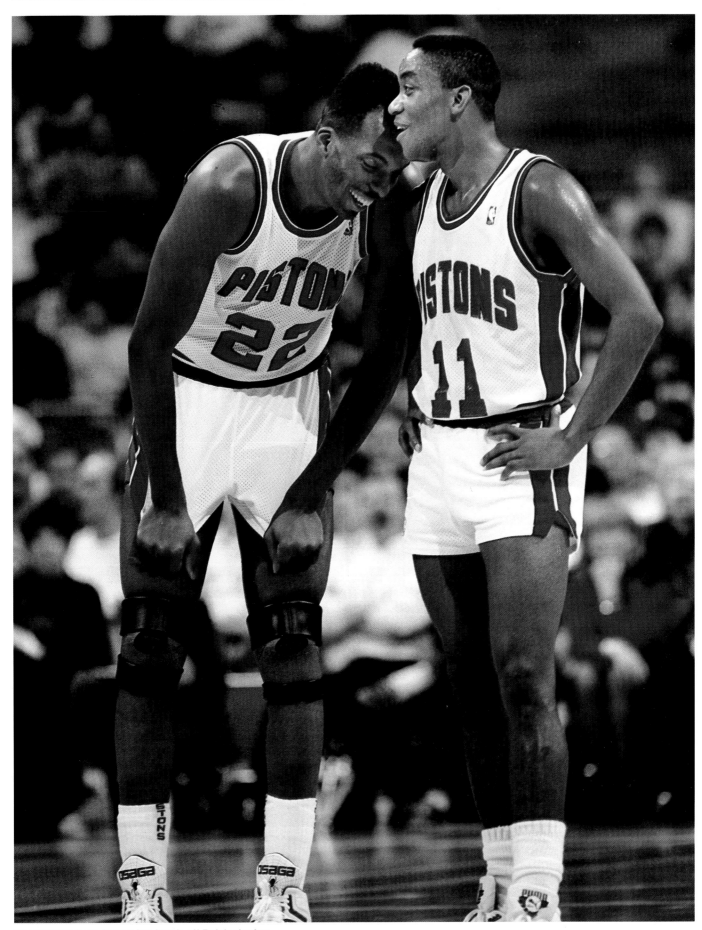

The Pistons have learned to laugh off Daly's tirades.

Rollins, the veteran out of Clemson who spent most of his career with Atlanta before moving to Cleveland two seasons ago. Rollins has few offensive skills and is no rebounding demon. But he just may provide the frontcourt defensive help that Daly is looking for.

THE CIRCUS

The NBA is a players' game. Chuck Daly knows that more than anyone. Some days, he has the urge just to rule with the whistle, like he did back when he was a college coach. Just run his players for two or three hours to work out all the problems. But he knows that wouldn't do.

"I know it isn't feasible with this team, or in this league," he says.

Like Isiah Thomas, his point guard, Daly has had to compromise over the years. He has resisted his urges to overcoach, to push too hard. Insiders with the Lakers say that Pat Riley seemed to lose track of the notion that the NBA is a player's game. He pushed too hard and wore out his relationships with his players.

As Jerry West explained, you have to give your players, especially your point guard, enough freedom to be creative; you have to let 'em play.

Daly has allowed creativity and freedom. But even that doesn't mean all the personality conflicts and other problems go away.

"Let's be honest," Daly says. "When you've played as many games as we play and a person has to make as many demands as I do, you're not going to have a lot of so-called happy campers. You're gonna have guys who go up and down.

"John Salley and I had a shouting match in Cleveland on the bench on national television. No big deal. John handled it, and I handled it. The next day it was over. But I think that aspect of it is something you have to deal with."

Salley smiles at the mention of Daly. "He yells whether you're rightr or wrong anyway," Salley says. "I'm used to it."

"Keeping it together for seven

years with the same people—although they're not a lot of the same people—you can wear on each other," Daly says. "There's a high level of tolerance necessary to continue."

Tolerance means taking one thing at a time, being patient, relying on your sense of humor and your cool, and above all, realizing that you can't do it all with coaching.

"I think basically we have a good working relationship," Daly says of the team.

The challenge, then, is to maintain that relationship through the

Part of the Pistons' success will depend on how each player improves individually. In the past, they've all worked hard to get better.

upcoming heat, which Daly is confident he can do. He'll simply rely on his instincts. He has displayed a knack for knowing just when to let up, just when to push.

"I know so much about these players," he says. "I get lucky bringing them in and putting them out, but a lot of it has to do with the so-called local knowledge."

Most important, he knows what to expect of the upcoming season. And he knows what direction the Pistons must take.

"Everybody gets a little bit better," he says. "Everybody gets up a notch to play us. And we'll have to respond."

He has talked to his assistants, and they've formulated their ideas for the upcoming season. "We'd like to do a lot of things differently," he says. "But when you've got a successful formula, you've got to be careful about messing with it too much. We're not gonna go all passing game. I would like to see us pick up the pace a little bit. How we do that I don't know.

"I'd like to see us throw in a couple of more presses with our second unit, see if we can do that. But that's easy to say and hard to do when you're in our position."

Quite simply, pressure to win the home-court advantage in the playoffs cuts down on the Pistons' ability to experiment. And it places all the more importance on the exhibition season. They want to have their routine ironed out before they head into the regular schedule, simply because they don't want to stack up early losses that will hurt them at the end of the season.

Part of the Pistons' success will depend on how each player improves individually. In the past, they've all worked hard to get better. Isiah's ability to shoot threes was a major reason for their success in the 1990 Finals. But across the roster, each player added depth to his game. Salley bulked up and played more of a banging role. Aguirre focused on his defense and rebounding. Dumars took on more leadership in the offense. Laimbeer developed more confidence in his shot and even added some low-post scoring. Edwards worked harder defensively. Rodman pushed to improve his free-throw shooting.

More than likely, continued individual improvement will be the key to maintaining their lofty position in pro basketball.

A great team will have to get better.

Come to think of it, that's what Red always told his Celtics.

LAIMBEER

As the anchor to Detroit's low-post defense, Laimbeer is a key question mark for the team. How much longer will he play? He almost retired after the 1989 season when the Pistons lost Mahorn.

"I knew what a long, grinding season it was gonna be," he said. "We had lost a physical player, and all the physical responsibilities were going to fall on myself. I knew it would be a very long season for me."

Ultimately, Isiah talked him out of it.

"Basically he just said a couple of things," Laimbeer recalled. "One was money. And the second one was that I'd miss the cameraderie amongst the guys. I came to the conclusion that I couldn't bail out on 'em, 'cause they're what I play for. And they play for me."

Laimbeer has been particularly moved by Vinnie Johnson's team-oriented sacrifices. After the season, he thanked Johnson personally for everything he had done. "Vinnie Johnson could have been an All-Star if he played for a team where he is the go-to man," Laimbeer said during last year's Finals. "He has sacrificed his entire game throughout his whole career for the Detroit Piston organization, and he's one of my favorite individuals."

Another favorite is Isiah. The upcoming season will mark a decade they've spent together as the nucleus of the Pistons. "Isiah is a tremendous individual," Laimbeer says. "He's one of the smartest people I know. He's very perceptive; he's intelligent; and he's my friend."

At 33, Laimbeer is as durable as ever, and McCloskey scoffs at the notion that the center seriously contemplates retirement.

"That's a lot of crap," the general manager says. "Why would anybody in their right mind want to leave the opportunity to get lots of exercise for an hour or so a day and be paid astronomical amounts of money? Why would anybody want to leave that. That's not logical?"

At the same time, Chuck Daly

knows that Laimbeer needs help in the frontcourt.

"We have to bring a Bedford or someone along who can give us some solid minutes," Daly says. "Where that guy is, I don't know."

BLANKS

In hopes of finding a fourth guard, the Pistons drafted hotshot Lance Blanks out of the University of Texas as a first-rounder. He was not their first choice, McCloskey says. They had hoped for Dave Jamerson out of the University of Ohio or Willie Glass out of the University of Mississippi.

Laimbeer has been particularly moved by Vinnie Johnson's team-oriented sacrifices. After the season, he thanked Johnson personally for everything he had done.

They also liked Dee Brown of Jacksonville, who went to the Celtics.

At the same time, they're not at all displeased with their selection. Blanks has plenty of competitiveness, a big factor in Detroit's evaluations. The Pistons thought enough of him to sign him to a four-year contract.

"He's a competitor, and he's very skilled," McCloskey says. "He can play both positions reasonably well."

With Daly looking to have the

second unit pressing more, the 6'4" Blanks could see some decent minutes. That, of course, will depend on his continued hard work and his adjustment to the pro game.

BEDFORD

William Bedford may just be the answer to the big-man question mark in Detroit's future. McCloskey hopes so, and Daly isn't convinced yet. The coach did give the 7'1" center some minutes during last year's playoffs, but he wasn't entirely pleased with Bedford's defensive intensity.

"He's skilled, there's no question about it," McCloskey says. "He could be that young player that takes us over the hump. But again, he's got to show that kind of improvement."

To date, Bedford hasn't come near to realizing his potential. Substance-abuse treatment interrupted his early career, but he seems to have put those problems behind him.

Playing time will be essential to his development, but that may be difficult with the Pistons. "I think if he were with another team, an expansion team or something, he'd be a very established player in this league," McCloskey says.

But more playing time will depend on Bedford, McCloskey says. "If he shows Chuck that he deserves that time, he'll get it."

"He's going to get an opportunity," Daly says, "in camp and during the exhibition season to find out if he really wants to play on a night-to-night basis."

Circumstances are difficult for Bedford, McCloskey acknowledges. "He's got Edwards and Laimbeer and Salley and Rodman and Aguirre in front of him, and that makes it tough."

But at least he has a ring, the general manager says.

Even better, he's got a spot in Chuck Daly's Three-ring Circus.

Here's hoping that it's a really big show.

Piston Profiles

MARK AGUIRRE

Position: Forward
Height: 6'6"
Weight: 232
High School: Chicago Westinghouse
College: DePaul '82
Birthdate: 12-10-59
When Drafted: First overall, Dallas 1981 as a hardship
How Acquired: Acquired from the Dallas Mavericks on February 15 in the NBA's biggest and most controversial trade of the season
Pro Experience: Nine Years
Married: Angela
Children: Angelei
Residence: Bloomfield Hills, MI

LAST SEASON: In his first full season with the Pistons, he finished the campaign coming off the bench for the first time in his career... After beginning the season as the team's starting small forward, he moved to the bench on January 30... He started his first 39 games... Missed three games due to a lower back strain then returned only to come off the bench... Averaged 14.1 points per game both off the bench and as a starter... He scored 20 or more points in 16 games... His 14.1 points per game was a career low... Shot 51 percent from the field as a starter and 47 percent off the bench... During the season, he eclipsed the 15,000 points scored total... During the 1990 playoffs, he averaged 11.0 points per game... Started the final three games of the 1990 NBA Finals, all Pistons victories...

AS A PRO: Acquired from the Dallas Mavericks on February 15, 1989 in the NBA's biggest and most controversial trade of the season... While acquiring Aguirre, the Pistons sent Adrian Dantley and Detroit's 1991 number-one draft choice to the Dallas Mavericks... Including the playoffs, the Pistons were 45-8 with Aguirre, sporting a 44-6 record when he was in the starting lineup during that first year... Since he has been with the Pistons, the team has recorded a 119-36 record with two NBA World Championships... All-time leading scorer in Dallas Mavericks' history... In 1984 was the first-ever Maverick to play in an All-Star Game... Has now played in three mid-season classics... Holds Maverick records for points in a quarter (24), a half (32), points in a game (49) and a season (2,330)... Was the first player selected in the 1981 NBA draft, while fellow Chicagoan and Pistons' team captain Isiah Thomas was the second player selected in that same college draft...

AS A COLLEGIAN: Led Depaul to a 79-10 record in his three years while averaging 24.5 points per game... Two-time consensus All-American... Received several player of the year honors during the post-season of his sophomore and junior seasons... Played in the Final Four as a freshman... Left DePaul after his junior season... Played on the 1980 United States Olympic Team...

PERSONAL: In 1988, married the former Angela Bowman on All-Star Saturday in Chicago, his hometown... Included in his wedding party were Isiah Thomas and Magic Johnson... Was cut the first time he tried out for his grade school team... Avid golfer who plays nearly every day during the off-season...

NBA CAREER RECORD

TEAM-YR	GP	MIN	FGM	FGA	PCT	FTM	FTA	PCT	OFF	DEF	REB	AVE	AST	PF-DQ	ST	BL	PTS	AVE	HI
DAL.'82	51	1468	381	820	.465	168	247	.680	89	160	249	4.9	164	152-0	37	22	955	18.7	42
DAL.'83	81	2784	767	1589	.483	429	589	.728	191	317	508	6.3	332	247-5	80	26	1979	24.4	44
DAL.'84	79	2900	925	1765	.524	465	621	.749	161	308	469	5.9	358	246-5	80	22	2330	29.5	46
DAL.'85	80	2699	794	1569	.506	440	580	.759	188	289	477	6.0	249	250-3	60	24	2055	25.7	49
DAL.'86	74	2501	666	1327	.503	318	451	.705	177	268	445	6.0	339	229-6	62	14	1670	22.6	42
DAL.'87	80	2663	787	1590	.495	429	557	.770	181	246	427	5.3	254	243-4	84	30	2056	25.7	43
DAL.'88	77	2610	746	1571	.475	388	504	.770	182	252	434	5.6	278	223-1	70	57	1932	25.1	38
DL-DT '89	80	2597	586	1270	.461	288	393	.733	146	240	386	4.8	278	229-2	45	36	1511	18.9	41
DET.'90	78	2005	438	898	.487	192	254	.756	117	188	305	3.9	145	201-2	34	19	1099	14.1	31
TOTALS	680	22227	6090	12399	.491	3117	4196	.742	1432	2268	3700	5.4	4117	2020-28	552	250	15587	22.9	49

NBA HIGHS

14	20		9	10	15		17		5	3	49

3-POINT FIELD GOALS: 1981-82, 25-71 (.352); 1982-83, 16-76 (.211); 1983-84, 15-56 (.268); 1984-85, 27-85 (.318); 1985-86, 16-56 (.286); 1986-87, 53-150 (.353); 1987-88, 52-172 (.302); 1988-89, 51-174 (.293); 1989-90, 31-93 (.333).
CAREER: 286-933 (.306).

NBA PLAYOFF RECORD

TEAM-YR	GP	MIN	FGM	FGA	PCT	FTM	FTA	PCT	OFF	DEF	REB	AST	PF-DQ	ST	BL	PTS	AVE
DALL. '84	10	350	88	184	.478	44	57	.772	21	55	76	32	34- 2	5	5	220	22.0
DALL. '85	4	164	44	89	.494	27	32	.844	16	14	30	16	16- 1	3	0	116	29.0
DALL. '86	10	345	105	214	.491	35	55	.636	21	50	71	54	28- 1	9	0	247	24.7
DALL. '87	4	130	31	62	.500	23	30	.767	11	13	24	8	15- 1	8	0	85	21.3
DALL. '88	17	558	147	294	.500	60	86	.698	34	66	100	56	49- 0	14	9	367	21.6
DET. '89	17	462	89	182	.489	28	38	.737	26	49	75	28	38- 0	8	3	274	12.6
DET. '90	20	439	86	184	.467	39	52	.750	31	60	91	27	51- 0	10	3	219	11.0
TOTALS	82	2448	590	1209	.488	256	350	.731	160	307	467	221	231- 5	57	20	1309	15.9

PLAYOFF HIGHS

19	30	11	12		17	10		39

3-POINT FIELD GOALS: 1983-84, 0-5; 1984-85, 1-2 (.500); 1985-86, 2-6 (.333); 1986-87, 0-4; 1987-88, 13-34 (.382); 1988-89, 8-29 (.276); 1989-90, 8-24 (.333).
CAREER: 31-104 (.298).

NBA ALL-STAR RECORD

TEAM-YR	GP	MIN	FGM	FGA	PCT	FTM	FTA	PCT	OFF	DEF	REB	AST	PF-DQ	ST	BL	PTS	AVE
DALL '84	1	13	5	8	.625	3	4	.750	1	0	1	2	2- 0	1	1	13	13.0
DALL '87	1	17	3	6	.500	2	3	.667	1	1	2	1	1- 0	0	0	9	9.0
DALL '88	1	12	5	10	.500	3	3	1	0	1	1	1	3- O	1	0	14	14.0
TOTALS	3	42	13	24	.542	8	10	.800	2	2	4	4	6- 0	2	1	36	12.0

WILLIAM BEDFORD

Position: Center
Height: 7'1"
Weight: 252
High School: Melrose, Memphis, TN
College: Memphis State '87 (Criminal Justice Major)
Birthdate: 12-14-63
When Drafted: First Round (6th Overall) Phoenix, 1986
How Acquired: From Phoenix for the Pistons' Number-One Draft Pick in 1988
Pro Experience: Three Years
Married: Pamela
Children: Diaundra
Residence: Rochester Hills, MI

LAST SEASON: Returned to the Pistons in 1989-90 after missing all of the previous season... He played sparingly for much of the season, finishing the year by averaging 2.8 points in 42 contests... Shot just 43 percent from the field and 41 percent from the free-throw line... Recorded 40 games of DNPs due to Coach's Decision... Scored his season high of 13 points at Seattle on December 2...

AS A PRO: Did not play in any games with the Pistons during the 1988-89 season... Spent most of the year in the Adult Substance Abuse Program in Van Nuys, California... On March 30, 1988, he admitted to a drug-dependency problem... Played in just 38 games during his first season (1987-88) with the Pistons and averaged 2.7 points per game and 1.7 rebounds per contest... Acquired by the Pistons on June 21, 1987 from the Phoenix Suns for Detroit's number-one draft pick in the 1988 NBA draft... Had a very slow start with the Suns, then suffered torn knee ligaments and had arthroscopic surgery in October of 1986... Entered the NBA after his junior season...

AS A COLLEGIAN: Named third team All-America by the Associated Press and was first team All-Metro Conference in 1986... Finished second behind Keith Lee with 234 career blocked shots at Memphis State... In 1986, he led the Tigers in scoring (17.3), rebounding (8.5), field-goal percentage (.584) and blocked shots (86)... Enjoyed career highs of 30 points and 18 rebounds versus Middle Tennessee State in 1986... Sports Illustrated rated him the number-one true center in the 1986 NBA college draft... Memphis State qualified for the NCAA tournament all three seasons he was there, including one trip to the Final Four... Memphis State was 85-17 during his three-year career...

PERSONAL: Married just prior to the start of the 1987-88 Pistons season to the former Pamela Hicks... Born December 14, 1963 in Memphis, Tennessee... Has three sisters... At Memphis State, he majored in Criminal Justice and was a member of the Phi Beta Sigma fraternity... Needs one year to complete his degree requirements...

NBA CAREER RECORD

TEAM-YR	GP	MIN	FGM	FGA	PCT	FTM	FTA	PCT	OFF	DEF	REB	AVE	AST	PF-DQ	STE	BLO	PTS	AVE	HI
PHO.'87	50	979	142	358	.397	50	86	.581	79	167	246	4.9	57	125- 1	18	37	334	6.7	17
DET.'88	38	298	44	101	.436	13	23	.565	27	38	65	1.7	4	47- 0	8	17	101	2.7	14
DET.'90	42	246	54	125	.432	9	22	.409	15	43	58	1.4	4	39- 0	3	17	118	2.8	13
TOTALS	130	1523	240	584	.411	72	131	.550	121	248	369	2.8	65	211- 1	29	71	553	4.3	17

NBA HIGHS

	34		6	16		6	8		6	8	12		3		3	4	17	

NBA PLAYOFF RECORD

TEAM-YR	GP	MIN	FGM	FGA	PCT	FTM	FTA	PCT	OFF	DEF	REB	AST	PF-DQ	ST	BL	PTS	AVE
DET. '90	5	19	1	6	.167	2	2	1	0	2	2	0	4- 0	0	1	4	0.8

PLAYOFF HIGHS

	7	1	4		2	2		2	2			1	2

JOE DUMARS

Position: Guard
Height: 6'3"
Weight: 195
College: McNeese State '85 (Business Management Major)
High School: Natchitoches-Central (LA)
Birthdate: 5/24/63
Birthplace: Natchitoches, LA
When Drafted: First Round (18th Overall) Detroit, 1985
How Acquired: College Draft
Pro Experience: Five Years
Married: Debbie
Residence: Burmingham, MI

LAST SEASON: Had the best season of his career, culminating in his first NBA All-Star Game appearance... For the second straight season, he was selected NBA First Team All Defense... Each year he's been in the league his scoring average has increased and 1989-90 was the same story... He finished the campaign by averaging 17.8 points per game... For the second straight season, though, he broke his left hand... Broke his left hand at San Antonio on March 24 and was expected to miss four weeks... He returned in just 16 days and missed seven games... In the first 68 games of the season, he averaged 18.4 points per game... Returned to the lineup after injury and came off the bench for the first four games... In the final seven games of the regular season after the injury he averaged 11.6 points per game... Shot a career-best 90 percent from the free-throw line, among the league leaders all season... Scored 20 or more points in 26 games... During the 1990 NBA playoffs, he averaged 18.2 points per game...

AS A PRO: No longer considered one of the league's most underrated guards... Named the Most Valuable Player in the 1989 NBA Finals, leading the Pistons to the first of two NBA

Championships... In the 1989 Finals he led Detroit with a 27.3 points per game average in the four-game sweep of the Lakers... Named to the NBA's First Team All Defense, joining teammate Dennis Rodman... Scored his career high of 42 points on April 12. 1989 in Cleveland as Detroit clinched the Central Division title... In that game, he scored 24 points in the third quarter, tying the all-time club record for points in a quarter... Also, he scored 17 straight points, the second most consecutive points total scored in Pistons' history... For the first time in his career, he had a serious injury which sidelined him for an extended period of time during the 1988-89 season... Broke his left hand versus New York on January 12, 1988 and had surgery two days later..After being inserted into the starting lineup during the middle of his rookie season, he has remained the team's starting off-guard since that time... Named to the NBA All-Rookie first team in 1985-86...

AS A COLLEGIAN: Four-time All-Southland Conference selection... Southland Conference leading scorer in 1982, 1984 and 1985... Ranked sixth in the nation in scoring in 1984, averaging 26.4 points per game... All-time McNeese State scoring leader... Holds virtually every McNeese State scoring record... Finished his collegiate career with a 22.3 scoring average... Played in the 1984 U.S. Olympic Trials... Second, all-time Southland Conference scoring leader behind Dwight Lamar... Still ranks among the nation's top 20 all-time leading scorers...

PERSONAL: Older brother David played pro football in the now defunct United States Football League... Comes from a football-oriented family... Has five brothers and one sister... In the 1984-85 McNeese State Media Guide, he listed his favorite athlete as the Pistons' Isiah Thomas... Married in September of 1989 to the former Debbie Nelson...

NBA CAREER RECORD

TEAM-YR	GP	MIN	FGM	FGA	PCT	FTM	FTA	PCT	OFF	DEF	REB	AVE	AST	PF-DQ	ST	BL	PTS	AVE	HI
DET.'86	82	1957	287	597	.481	190	238	.798	60	59	119	1.4	390	200-1	66	11	769	9.4	22
DET.'87	79	2439	369	749	.493	184	246	.748	50	117	167	2.1	352	194-1	83	5	931	11.8	24
DET.'88	82	2732	453	960	.472	251	308	.815	63	137	200	2.4	387	155-1	87	15	1161	14.1	25
DET.'89	69	2408	456	903	.505	260	306	.849	57	115	172	2.5	390	103-1	63	5	1186	17.2	42
DET.'90	75	2578	508	1058	.480	297	330	.900	60	152	212	2.8	368	129- 1	63	2	1335	17.8	34
TOTALS	387	12114	2073	4267	.486	1182	1428	.828	290	580	870	2.24	806	781- 5	362	38	5382	13.9	42

NBA HIGHS

| | 53 | 18 | 24 | | 18 | 19 | | 5 | 8 | 10 | | 14 | | 5 | 2 | 42 | |

3-POINT FIELD GOALS: 1985-86, 5-16 (.313); 1986-87, 9-22 (.409); 1987-88, 4-19 (.210); 1988-89, 14-29 (.483); 1989-90, 22-55 (.400).
CAREER: 51-141 (.383).

NBA PLAYOFF RECORD

TEAM-YR	GP	MIN	FGM	FGA	PCT	FTM	FTA	PCT	OFF	DEF	REB	AST	PF-DQ	ST	BL	PTS	AVE
DET.'86	4	147	25	41	.610	10	15	.667	6	7	13	25	16-0	4	0	60	15.0
DET.'87	15	473	78	145	.538	32	41	.780	8	11	19	72	126-0	12	1	190	12.7
DET.'88	23	804	113	247	.457	56	63	.889	18	32	50	112	50-1	13	2	284	12.3
DET.'89	17	620	106	233	.455	87	101	.861	11	33	44	96	31-0	12	1	300	17.6
DET.'90	20	754	130	284	.453	99	113	.876	18	26	44	95	37- 0	22	0	364	18.2
TOTALS	79	2798	452	950	.476	284	333	.853	61	109	170	400	160- 1	63	4	1198	15.1

PLAYOFF HIGHS

| | 15 | 23 | | 13 | 17 | | | | | 7 | 11 | | | | 35 | |

3-POINT FIELD GOALS: 1986-87, 2-3 (.667); 1987-88, 2-6 (.333); 1988-89, 1-12 (.083), 1989-90, 5-19 (.263).
CAREER: 10-40 (.250).

NBA ALL-STAR RECORD

TEAM-YR	GP	MIN	FGM	FGA	PCT	FTM	FTA	PCT	OFF	DEF	REB	AST	PF-DQ	ST	BL	PTS	AVE
DET. '90	1	18	3	4	.750	1	2	.500	0	1	1	5	0- 0	0	0	9	9

JAMES EDWARDS

Position: Center
Height: 7'1"
Weight: 252
College: Washington, '77
High School: Roosevelt, Seattle, WA
Birthdate: 11/22/55
Birthplace: Seattle, WA
When Drafted: Third Round (46th pick) Los Angeles, 1977
How Acquired: From Phoenix Suns in exchange for Ron Moore and Detroit's Second-Round Draft Choice in 1991
Pro Experience: 13 Years
Marital Status: Single
Residence: Phoenix, AZ

LAST SEASON: Was the biggest surprise of the 1989-90 regular season... Opened the campaign coming off the bench, he was moved into the starting lineup by Coach Chuck Daly after just 12 games into the season... He started the final 70 games of the regular season, during which time the Pistons were 52-18... His scoring average as a reserve was 5.7 points per game... As a starter he averaged 16.0 points per game... As a starter he recorded double-figure scoring efforts in 61 of 70 games... By averaging 14.5 points per game in the 1989-90 season, he's now averaged double figures in 12 of his 13 campaigns... He scored 20 or more points in 21 games, all as a starter... His 2,283 minutes played were the most in the last eight seasons... Played every game during the regular season for only the fourth time in his 13 seasons, not missing any games due to injury... Shot 75 percent from the free-throw

line, his second highest percentage of his career... In the 1990 playoffs, he averaged 14.3 points per game, including a playoff career high of 32 points against the Knicks in the second round...

AS A PRO: The Pistons have now played in the NBA Finals in each of his three seasons with Detroit... Acquired from the Phoenix Suns on February 24, 1988 in exchange for Ron Moore and a second-round draft choice... Played in 26 regular-season games with the Pistons that year... Averaged 5.4 points and 3.0 rebounds during the remainder of the season with the Pistons... Prior to that, he played in 43 games with Phoenix and averaged 15.5 points and 7.8 rebounds... Then, in his first full season with the Pistons (1988-89), he did not average double figures for the first time in his career... Was a member of the Cleveland Cavaliers in 1981-82 when Chuck Daly was the coach... Ironically, at that time, Edwards was the starting center, while Bill Laimbeer was the backup... Eclipsed the 10,000 career point total during the 1987-88 campaign... Originally drafted by the Los Angeles Lakers in the 3rd round of the 1977 NBA Draft...

AS A COLLEGIAN: An All-Pac 8 performer at the University of Washington, finished as the school's second-leading all-time scorer with 1,548 points... Scored a collegiate high of 37 points in his junior year against Oregon State... Averaged 20.9 points and 10.4 rebounds as a senior...

PERSONAL: Makes his year-round home in West Bloomfield... Became heavily involved with several charities while in Phoenix and expects to do the same here in Detroit... He is a boating expert...

NBA CAREER RECORD

TEAM-YR	GP	MIN	FGM	FGA	PCT	FTM	FTA	PCT	OFF	DEF	REB	AVE	AST	PF-DQ	STE	BLO	PTS	AVE
LA-IN.'78	83	2405	495	1093	.453	272	421	.646	197	418	615	7.4	85	322-12	53	78	1262	15.2
IND.'79	82	2546	534	1065	.501	298	441	.676	179	514	693	8.5	92	363-16	60	109	1366	16.7
IND.'80	82	2314	528	1032	.512	231	339	.681	179	399	578	7.0	127	324-12	55	104	1287	15.7
IND.'81	81	2375	511	1004	.509	244	347	.703	191	380	571	7.0	212	304- 7	32	128	1266	15.6
CLV.'82	77	2539	528	1033	.511	232	339	.684	189	392	581	7.5	123	347-17	24	117	1288	16.7
CL-PH.'83	31	667	128	263	.487	69	108	.639	56	99	155	5.0	40	110- 5	12	19	325	10.5
PHO.'84	72	1897	438	817	.536	183	254	.720	108	240	348	4.8	184	254- 3	23	30	1059	14.7
PHO.'85	70	1787	384	766	.501	276	370	.746	95	292	387	5.5	153	237- 5	26	52	1044	14.9
PHO.'86	52	1314	318	587	.542	212	302	.702	79	222	301	5.8	74	200- 5	23	29	848	16.3
PHO.'87	14	304	57	110	.518	54	70	.771	20	40	60	4.3	19	42- 1	6	7	168	12.0
DET.'89	76	1254	211	422	.500	133	194	.685	68	163	231	3.0	49	226- 1	11	31	555	7.3
DET.'90	82	2283	462	928	.498	265	354	.748	112	233	345	4.2	63	295- 4	37	23	1189	14.5
TOTALS	871	23390	4896	9763	.501	2679	3860	.694	1592	3685	5277	6.0	1299	3240-90	778	764	12471	14.3

NBA HIGHS

| | 16 | 29 | 18 | 19 | | 18 | | 7 | | | | | 7 | 39 | | | | |

3-POINT FIELD GOALS: 1979-80, 0-1 (.000); 1980-81, 0-3 (.000); 1981-82, 0-4 (.000); 1983-84, 0-1 (.000); 1984-85, 0-3 (.000); 1987-88, 0-1 (.000); 1988-89, 0-2 (.000); 1989-90, 0-3 (.000).
CAREER: 0-18 (.000)

NBA PLAYOFF RECORD

TEAM-YR	GP	MIN	FGM	FGA	PCT	FTM	FTA	PCT	OFF	DEF	REB	AST	PF-DQ	ST	BL	PTS	AVE
IND. '81	2	56	7	24	.292	0	0	.000	4	10	14	5	8-0	1	1	14	7.0
PHO.'83	3	7	11	26	.423	6	6	1.000	6	12	18	4	7-0	1	1	28	9.3
PHO.'84	17	463	93	189	.492	48	68	.706	22	69	91	27	62-3	4	11	234	13.8
DET.'88	22	308	56	110	.509	27	41	.659	23	45	68	11	55-0	2	10	139	6.3
DET.'89	17	317	40	85	.471	40	51	.784	11	25	36	12	53-0	1	8	120	7.1
DET.'90	20	536	114	231	.494	58	96	.604	24	47	71	13	74- 0	5	11	286	14.3
TOTALS	81	1734	321	665	.483	179	262	.683	90	208	298	72	259 -3	14	42	821	10.1

PLAYOFF HIGHS

| | | 13 | 23 | | 9 | 10 | | | | 9 | 4 | | | | 32 | |

3-POINT FIELD GOALS: 1987-88, 0-1; 1988-89, 0-1; 1989-90, 0-1 (.000).
CAREER: 0-3 (.000).

SCOTT HASTINGS

Position: Forward/Center
Height: 6'11"
Weight: 245
College: '82 Arkansas (Public Relations)
High School: Independence High School (KS)
Birthdate: 6/3/60
Birthplace: Independence, KS
When Drafted: New York, 1982 2nd round (29th overall)
How Acquired: Free Agent (Formerly with Miami Heat)
Pro Experience: Eight Years
Married: Judy
Children: Ashley, Allison
Residence: Roswell, GA

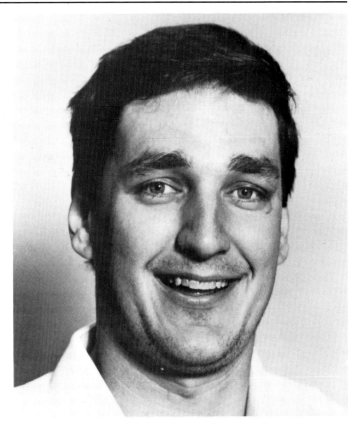

LAST SEASON: Signed as an unrestricted free agent by the Pistons on July 17, 1989... Played in a total of 40 games with the Pistons during 1989-90 and averaged 1.1 points per game... Had 40 DNPs due to coach's decision, and one game missed due to suspension... Played double-figure minutes in four games all season... His best game was in the season-opener against the Knicks with 9 points in 15 minutes on November 3...

AS A PRO: Prior to signing with the Pistons, he played for the expansion Miami Heat in 1988-89, averaging 5.1 points per game in 75 appearances... Eight-year NBA veteran began his career with the New York Knicks... Traded during the middle of his rookie season and played the next five and one-half seasons with the Atlanta Hawks... Was then acquired by Miami in the 1988 NBA expansion draft... Original second-round draft choice of the Knicks (29th overall) in 1982... Traded along with $600,000 to Atlanta for Rory Sparrow in February of 1983...

AS A COLLEGIAN: Honorable mention All-American during his senior season at Arkansas... Left Arkansas as the second leading all-time scorer behind only Sidney Moncrief... Led Razorbacks in scoring during his sophomore, junior and senior seasons...

PERSONAL: Conducts his own basketball camp in Kansas during the off-season... Avid golfer... Also won high school letters in both tennis and football... Kansas Player-of-the-Year as a senior... Majored in Public Relations in college... Scott and wife Judy are parents of two daughters Ashley and Allison...

NBA CAREER RECORD

TEAM-YR	GP	MIN	FGM	FGA	PCT	FTM	FTA	PCT.	OFF	DEF	REB	AVE	AST	PF-DQ	STE	BLO	PTS	AVE
NY-ATL'83	31	140	13	38	.342	11	20	.550	15	26	41	1.3	3	34- 0	6	1	37	1.2
ATL. '84	68	1135	111	237	.488	82	104	.788	96	174	270	3.9	46	220- 7	40	38	305	4.5
ATL. '85	64	825	89	188	.473	63	81	.778	59	100	159	2.4	46	135- 1	24	23	241	3.8
ATL. '86	62	650	65	159	.409	60	70	.857	44	80	124	2	26	118- 2	14	8	193	3.1
ATL. '87	40	256	23	68	.338	23	29	.783	16	54	70	1.8	13	35- 0	10	7	71	1.8
ATL. '88	55	403	40	82	.488	25	27	.926	27	70	97	1.8	16	67- 1	8	10	110	2.0
MIAMI'89	75	1206	143	328	.436	91	107	.850	72	159	231	3.1	59	203- 5	32	42	386	5.1
DET. '90	40	166	10	33	.303	19	22	.864	7	25	32	0.8	8	31- 0	3	31	42	1.1
TOTALS	435	4781	494	1133	.436	374	460	.813	336	688	1024	2.3	217	843-16	137	160	1385	3.2

NBA HIGHS

	41					9	10				17	6			3	3	17	

3-POINT FIELD GOALS: 1985-86, 1-4 (.250); 1987-88, 0-1 (.000); 1988-89, 9-28 (.321); 1989-90, 3-12 (.250). CAREER: 23-75 (.307).

NBA PLAYOFF RECORD

TEAM-YR	GP	MIN	FGM	FGA	PCT	FTM	FTA	PCT	OFF	DEF	REBS	AVE	AST	PF-DQ	STE	BLO	PTS.	AVE
ATL. '84	5	32	2	9	.222	3	4	.750	2	6	8	1.6	1	4- 0	1	0	7	1.4
ATL. '86	9	49	11	14	.786	5	11	.455	3	7	10	1.1	2	11- 0	2	0	28	3.1
ATL. '87	4	21	2	3	.667	2	2	1	1	5	6	1.5	0	5- 0	1	1	6	1.5
ATL. '88	11	103	9	14	.643	8	8	1	7	10	17	1.5	3	21- 1	3	1	26	2.4
DET. '90	5	16	1	4	.250	0	0	.000	0	0	0	0	0	4- 0	1	0	2	0.4
TOTALS	34	221	25	44	.568	18	25	.720	13	28	41	1.2	6	45- 1	8	2	69	20.2

PLAYOFF HIGHS

	15	4	5		4	5		2	3	4		1			2	0	10	

VINNIE JOHNSON

Position: Guard
Height: 6'2"
Weight: 200
College: Baylor '79 (Education Major)
High School: F.D. Roosevelt (Brooklyn, NY)
Birthdate: 9/1/56
Birthplace: Brooklyn, NY
When Drafted: First Round (7th Overall) Seattle, 1979
How Acquired: In Exchange for Greg Kelser, Nov. 21, 1981
Pro Experience: 11 Years
Nickname: V.J.
Marital Status: Single
Residence: Southfield, MI

LAST SEASON: Hit the game-winning jump shot in the decisive Game Five of the NBA Finals against Portland... Connected on a 15-footer with 0.07 seconds remaining in the contests and gave Detroit its second straight World Championship... Averaged 12.2 points per game in the Finals... For the second straight regular season, he came out of his scoring slump at the end of the season, finishing at 9.8 points per game... But, for the first time since he joined the Pistons, he did not average double figures... Eclipsed the 10,000 career point total in 1989-90... With the injury to Dumars, he started 11 straight games and during that time he averaged 15.8 points, 6.4 rebounds and 4.5 assists... Scored better than double figures in 17 of the final 19 games of the regular season... Missed most of training camp due to a broken rib... For the third straight season, he played in every game...

AS A PRO: Ranks on many of the Pistons' top 10 categories of all-time career leaders including points, steals and games played... Tied with Isiah Thomas for most games played by a Piston (716) entering the 1990-91 season... Had probably his best season as a pro during the 1986-87 season when he was runner-up in the balloting for the NBA's Sixth Man Award... For most of the past five seasons, he has joined Dumars and Thomas in Coach Chuck Daly's three-guard rotation... Owns the Pistons' record for consecutive points scored when he burned Utah for 19 straight points on March 1, 1989... Acquired by the Pistons on November 21, 1981 from the Seattle SuperSonics in exchange for Gregory Kelser... Had one strong season in Seattle in 1980-81 when he started 63 games as Gus Williams sat the year out... Was the NBA's top offensive rebounder in that season, averaging 2.4 offensive boards per game...

AS A COLLEGIAN: Played at Baylor after transferring from McLennon Junior College in Waco, Texas after his sophomore season... Was the Southwest Conference leading scorer his senior season, averaging 25.2 points per game... During his two-year stay at Baylor, he was named to the Associated Press' All-America second team twice and became the school's second all-time leading scorer...

PERSONAL: Was dubbed the "Microwave" by former Celtic and current Trail Blazer Danny Ainge a few seasons ago, because V.J. heats up in a hurry... Vinnie is the middle child of four brothers and three sisters... His younger brother Eric played for the Utah Jazz last season... Makes his year-round home in Southfield...

NBA CAREER RECORD

TEAM-YR	GP	MIN	FGM	FGA	PCT	FTM	FTA	PCT	OFF	DEF	REB	AVE	AST	PF-DQ	ST	BLO	PTS	AVE	HI
SEA.'80	38	325	45	115	.391	31	39	.795	19	36	55	1.4	54	40-0	19	4	121	3.2	12
SEA.'81	81	2311	419	785	.534	214	270	.793	193	173	366	4.5	341	198-0	78	20	1053	13.0	31
SE-D'82	74	1295	217	444	.489	107	142	.754	82	77	159	2.1	171	101-0	56	25	544	7.4	20
DET.'83	82	2511	520	1013	.513	245	315	.778	167	186	353	4.3	301	263-2	93	49	1296	15.8	33
DET.'84	82	1909	426	901	.473	207	275	.753	130	107	237	2.9	271	196-1	44	19	1063	13.0	28
DET.'85	82	2093	428	942	.454	190	247	.769	134	118	252	3.1	325	205-2	71	20	1051	12.8	28
DET.'86	79	1978	465	996	.467	165	214	.771	119	107	226	2.9	269	180-2	80	23	1097	13.9	35
DET.'87	78	2166	533	1154	.462	158	201	.786	123	134	257	3.3	300	159-0	92	16	1228	15.7	30
DET.'88	82	1935	425	959	.443	147	217	.677	90	141	231	2.8	267	164-0	58	18	1002	12.2	28
DET.'89	82	2073	462	996	.464	193	263	.734	109	146	255	3.1	242	155-0	74	17	1130	13.8	34
DET.'90	82	1972	334	775	.431	131	196	.668	108	148	256	3.1	255	143-0	71	13	804	9.8	25
TOTALS	842	20568	4274	9080	.471	1788	2379	.752	1274	1373	2647	3.1	2796	1804-7	736	224	10389	12.3	35

NBA HIGHS

46	16	25		11	12		8	6	12		15		5	3	35

3-POINT FIELD GOALS: 1979-80, 0-1 (.000); 1980-81, 1-5 (.200); 1981-82, 3-12 (.250); 1982-83, 11-40 (.275); 1983-84, 4-19 (.211); 1984-85, 5-27 (.185); 1985-86, 2-14 (.143); 1986-87, 4-14 (.286); 1987-88, 5-24 (.208); 1988-89, 13-44 (.295); 1989-90, 5-34 (.147).
CAREER: 53-234 (.226).

NBA PLAYOFF RECORD

TEAM-YR	GP	MIN	FGM	FGA	PCT	FTM	FTA	PCT	OFF	DEF	REB	AST	PF-DQ	ST	BL	PTS	AVE
SEA.'80	5	12	1	3	.333	0	0	—	0	2	2	2	1-0	1	0	2	0.4
DET.'84	5	132	17	46	.370	17	19	.895	5	9	14	12	9-0	1	1	51	10.2
DET.'85	9	235	53	103	.515	22	28	.786	15	12	27	29	24-0	6	1	128	14.2
DET.'86	4	85	22	49	.449	7	13	.538	8	9	17	11	9-0	3	0	51	12.8
DET.'87	15	388	95	207	.459	31	36	.861	20	24	44	62	33-0	9	4	221	14.7
DET.'88	23	477	101	239	.423	33	50	.660	35	40	75	43	48-0	17	4	236	10.3
DET.'89	17	620	106	200	.455	87	101	.861	11	33	44	96	31-0	12	1	300	17.6
DET.'90	20	463	85	184	.462	34	43	.791	28	28	56	54	38-0	8	4	206	10.3
TOTALS	98	2164	465	1031	.451	191	251	.761	127	153	280	256	194-0	49	17	1134	11.5

PLAYOFF HIGHS

16	21	10	13		12	13	34

3-POINT FIELD GOALS: 1983-84, 0-1 (.000); 1984-85, 0-3 (.000); 1985-86, 0-1 (.000); 1986-87, 0-2 (.000); 1987-88, 1-7 (.143); 1988-89, 10-24 (.417); 1989-90. 2-7 (.286).
CAREER: 13-45 (.289).

BILL LAIMBEER

Position: Center
Height: 6'11"
Weight: 245
College: Notre Dame (Degree in Economics)
High School: Palos Verdes, CA
Birthdate: 5/19/57
Birthplace: Boston, MA
When Drafted: Third Round (65th Overall) Cleveland, 1979
How Acquired: From Cleveland with Kenny Carr for Phil Hubbard, Paul Mokeski, 1982 First Round Draft Choice, 1982 Second Round Draft Choice
Pro Experience: 10 Years
Nickname: Lambs
Married: Chris (1979)
Children: Eric William and Keriann
Residence: Orchard Lake, MI

LAST SEASON: Pistons' starting center averaged 12.1 points and 9.6 rebounds per game...Had an outstanding NBA Finals against Portland when he averaged 13.2 points and 13.4 rebounds...Tied an NBA Finals' record by connecting on six three-pointers against the Blazers in Game Two...For the second straight regular season he missed a game due to suspension...In his career, he's missed just three games, two due to suspension and one due to Coach's Decision...Had one of his best games of his career against Phoenix on January 26 when he scored 31 points and grabbed 23 rebounds...Set career highs with 57-158 on three-pointers...Had 31 games of double figures in points and rebounds...Was the Pistons' leading rebounder for seven straight seasons, before losing the team title to Dennis Rodman in 1989-90...

AS A PRO: Will become the all-time Pistons' leader in rebounding.sometime during the 1990-91 campaign...Needs just 296 rebounds to surpass Bob Lanier as the Pistons' all-time leading rebounder...
Had his Iron Man streak snapped at 685 straight games played, fourth longest in NBA

history when he was suspended for fighting during the 1988-89 season...The streak came to a halt due to a league-imposed, one-game suspension after a fight with Cleveland's Brad Daugherty...Twice he's grabbed 9 defensive rebounds in a quarter, an all-time Pistons' record...Has now averaged better than double figures in points in eight straight seasons...Went over the 10,000 career point total during the season 1988-89 season...Ranks in the top 10 of seven Pistons' all-time statistical categories...Came to the Pistons from Cleveland along with Kenny Carr in a deal that was made 9 minutes prior to the NBA trading deadline on Feb. 16, 1982...Started his first game with the Pistons and every one since...After not scoring 1,000 points in either of his first two NBA seasons, he's now surpassed 1,000 points in the next six season before just missing that total this year..Spent the 1979-80 in Italy (22 points per game) after being drafted by Cleveland in the third round of the 1979 NBA draft...Has been named to the NBA All-Star Team four times...Won the NBA rebounding title in 1985-86 when he averaged a career best 13.1 rebounds per game...

AS A COLLEGIAN: College teammate of former Piston Kelly Tripucka when the two were at Notre Dame...Made one appearance in the Final Four...As a senior at Notre Dame, his team was eliminated by eventual NCAA Champion Michigan State...

PERSONAL: High School All-American and two-time All-State pick in California...Played baseball and football in high school...In golf, has a one handicap and was the winner of the Cleveland Chapter of the NFL Alumni Association Golf Outing in 1982...Has organized the Bill Laimbeer 7-Eleven Muscular Dystrophy Golf Tournament each of the last six summers...Last summer, the event raised nearly $70,000 for MDA...Would love to play tournament golf when his playing days are complete...Played in the Celebrity Golf Classic in Lake Tahoe last Summer...In June, 1984, he signed a contract that will keep him in Detroit through the 1990 season...He and his wife Chris are the parents of two children Eric and Keriann...

NBA CAREER RECORD

TEAM-YR	GP	MIN	FGM	FGA	PCT	FTM	FTA	PCT	OFF	DEF	REB	AVE	AST	PF-DQ	ST	BLO	PTS	AVE	HI
CLE.'81	81	2460	337	670	.503	117	153	.765	266	427	693	8.6	216	332-1	456	78	791	9.8	26
CL-D'82	80	1829	265	36	.494	184	232	.793	234	383	617	7.7	100	296-5	39	64	718	9.0	30
DET.'83	82	2871	436	877	.497	245	310	.790	282	711	993	12.1	263	320-9	51	118	1119	13.6	30
DET.'84	82	2864	553	1044	.530	316	365	.866	329	674	1003	12.2	149	273-4	49	84	1422	17.3	33
DET.'85	82	2892	595	1177	.506	244	306	.797	295	718	1013	12.4	154	308-4	69	71	1438	17.5	35
DET.'86	82	2891	545	1107	.492	266	319	.834	305	770	1075	13.1	146	291-4	59	65	1360	16.6	29
DET.'87	82	2854	506	1010	.501	245	274	.894	243	712	955	11.6	151	283-4	72	69	1263	15.4	30
DET.'88	82	2897	455	923	.493	187	214	.874	165	667	832	10.1	199	284-6	66	78	1110	13.5	30
DET.'89	81	2640	449	900	.499	178	212	.840	138	638	776	9.6	177	259-2	51	100	1106	13.6	32
DET.'90	81	2675	380	785	.484	164	192	.854	166	614	780	9.6	171	278-4	57	84	981	12.1	31
TOTALS	815	26873	4521	9029	.500	2146	2577	.832	2423	6314	8737	10.7	1726	2925-56	569	811	11308	13.8	35

NBA HIGHS

51	16	27	12	13	12	20	24	11	5	6	35	

3-POINT FIELD GOALS: 1980-81, 0-0 (.000); 1981-82, 4-13 (.308); 1982-83, 2-13 (.154); 1983-84, 0-11 (.000); 1984-85, 4-18 (.222); 1985-86, 4-14 (.286); 1986-87, 6-21 (.286); 1987-88, 13-39 (.333), 1988-89, 30-86 (.349); 1989-90, 57-158 (.361).
CAREER: 118-373 (.316).

NBA PLAYOFF RECORD

TEAM-YR	GP	MIN	FGM	FGA	PCT	FTM	FTA	PCT	OFF	DEF	REB	AST	PF-DQ	ST	BL	PTS	AVE
DET.'84	5	165	29	51	.569	18	20	.900	14	48	62	12	23-2	4	3	76	15.2
DET.'85	9	325	48	107	.449	36	51	.706	36	60	96	15	32-1	7	7	132	14.7
DET.'86	4	168	34	68	.500	21	23	.913	20	36	56	1	19-1	2	3	90	22.5
DET.'87	15	543	84	163	.515	15	24	.625	30	126	156	37	53-2	15	12	184	12.3
DET.'88	23	779	114	250	.456	40	45	.889	43	178	221	44	77-2	18	19	273	11.9
DET.'89	17	497	66	142	.465	25	31	.806	26	114	140	31	55-1	6	8	172	10.1
DET.'90	20	667	91	199	.457	25	29	.862	41	170	211	28	77-3	23	18	222	11.1
TOTALS	93	3144	466	980	.476	180	223	.807	210	732	942	168	336-12	75	70	1149	12.4

PLAYOFF HIGHS

10	23	13	13	17	6	31	

3-POINT FIELD GOALS: 1984-85, 0-2 (.000); 1985-86, 1-1 (1.000); 1986-87, 1-5 (.200); 1987-88, 5-17 (.294); 1988-89, 15-42 (.357); 1989-90, 15-43 (.349).
CAREER: 47-110 (.427).

NBA ALL-STAR RECORD

TEAM-YR	GP	MINS	AVE	FGM	FGA	PCT	FTM	FTA	PCT	OFF	DEF	REB	AVE	AST	PF-DQ	ST	BL	PTS	AVE
DET.'83	1	6	6.0	1	1	1.000	0	0	.—	1	0	1	1.0	0	1-0	0	0	2	2.0
DET.'84	1	17	17.0	6	8	.750	1	1	1.000	1	4	5	5.0	0	3-0	1	2	13	13.0
DET.'85	1	11	11.0	2	4	.500	1	2	.500	1	2	3	3.0	1	1-0	0	0	5	5.0
DET.'87	1	11	11.0	4	7	.571	0	0	.—	0	2	2	2.0	1	1-2	1	0	8	8.0
TOTALS	4	45	11.3	13	20	.650	2	3	.667	3	8	11	2.8	2	7-0	2	2	28	7.0

DENNIS RODMAN

Position: Forward
Height: 6'8"
Weight: 210
College: Southeastern Oklahoma State '86
High School: South Oak Cliff HS (TX)
Birthdate: 05/13/61
Birthplace: Dallas, TX
When Drafted: Second Round (27th Overall) Detroit, 1986
How Acquired: College Draft
Pro Experience: Four Years
Nickname: Worm
Marital Status: Single
Residence: Dallas, TX

LAST SEASON: MasterLock NBA Defensive Player of the Year in 1989-90 and a first team All Defense unanimous selection... Played in his first NBA All-Star Game, scoring 4 points with 4 rebounds... For the regular season, he averaged 8.8 points and 9.6 rebounds... Connected on 58 percent from the field and shot a career-best 65 percent from the free-throw line... After again opening the season coming off the bench, he was moved into the starting lineup... Started the final 43 games of the regular season, during that time the Pistons were 34-9... Was one of the league's top offensive rebounders, grabbing 336 offensive boards, the highest of his career... Won the team rebounding title, ending Laimbeer's reign at seven straight seasons... Had 21 games of double figures in points and rebounds... For the second straight season, he recorded more rebounds than points scored...

AS A PRO: Two-time NBA All Defensive first team selection... In 1988-89 finished the season as the league's top field-goal percentage shooter, connecting on .595 of his attempts, shattering the all-time Pistons' record in the process... In 1988-89, finished second in the balloting for both the NBA's Defensive Player of the Year and the Sixth Man Award... Had his best game as a pro in Golden State on February 18, 1989 when he scored 32 points and grabbed 21 rebounds, both career highs... Has established himself as one of the NBA's top sixth men and offensive rebounders... Defensively, Coach Chuck Daly uses him at four positions... Has played in every game over the last three seasons... Entered the NBA from little-known Southeast Oklahoma State and made an impact with the Pistons immediately... Has been used at both forward positions, and at big guard... Connected on 57 percent of his field-goal attempts in his first four NBA seasons... Nicknamed Worm, he quickly became a fan favorite during his first year with the club... Has used Northwood Institute Coach Pat Miller as a shooting instructor over the past two seasons...

AS A COLLEGIAN: First Team NAIA All-American for three consecutive seasons... Did not play high school basketball and stood only 5'11" after his senior year... After graduation from high school, he grew 7 inches... Played one semester at Cooke County Junior College before transferring... Had 24 points and 19 rebounds in his first collegiate game, then followed with 40 points in his second game... As a sophomore, he scored 42 points and grabbed 24 rebounds in the semi-finals of the District Nine playoffs... Scored a career high of 51 points against Bethany Nazarene in the playoffs...

PERSONAL: His two sisters, Debra and Kim were High School All-Americans and led South Oak Cliff to two state titles... Debra, 6'3", went on to Louisiana Tech, played on a national championship team and was a three-time All-American... Kim was an All-American at Stephen F. Austin... Needless to say, his two sisters influenced him tremendously... An outstanding pinball player... Runs a very successful summer basketball camp...

NBA CAREER RECORD

TEAM-YR	GP	MIN	FGM	FGA	PCT	FTM	FTA	PCT.	OFF	DEF	REB	AVE	AST	PF-DQ	ST	BL	PTS	AVE	HI
DET.'87	77	1155	213	391	.545	74	126	.587	163	169	332	4.3	56	166-1	38	48	500	6.5	21
DET.'88	82	2147	398	709	.561	152	284	.535	318	397	715	8.7	110	273-5	75	45	953	11.6	30
DET.'89	82	2208	316	531	.595	97	155	.626	327	445	772	9.4	99	292- 4	55	76	735	9.0	32
DET.'90	82	2377	288	496	.581	142	217	.654	336	456	792	9.6	72	276- 2	52	60	719	8.8	18
TOTALS	323	7887	1215	2127	.571	465	782	.595	1144	1467	2611	8.0	359	1331263 37 1007-12	220	229	2907	9	32

NBA HIGHS

	43	13	17		9	11		10	13	21		5			4	4	32	

3-POINT FIELD GOALS: 1986-87, 0-1 (.000); 1987-88, 5-17 (.294); 1988-89, 6-26 (.231); 1989-90, 1-9 (.111).
CAREER: 12-53 (.226).

NBA PLAYOFF RECORD

TEAM-YR	GP	MIN	FGM	FGA	PCT	FTM	FTA	PCT	OFF	DEF	REB	AST	PF-DQ	ST	BL	PTS	AVE
DET.'87	15	245	40	74	.541	18	32	.563	32	39	71	3	48-0	6	17	98	6.5
DET.'88	23	474	71	136	.522	22	54	.407	51	85	136	21	87-1	14	14	164	7.1
DET.'89	17	409	37	70	.529	24	35	.686	56	114	170	16	58-0	6	12	198	5.8
DET. '90	19	560	54	95	.568	18	35	.514	55	106	161	17	62- 1	9	13	126	6.6
TOTALS	74	1688	202	375	.539	82	156	.526	194	344	538	57	255- 2	35	56	586	7.9

PLAYOFF HIGHS

	10	16		6	10				20		3				23	

3-POINT FIELD GOALS: 1987-88, 0-2 (.000); 1988-89, 0-4 (.000); 1989-90, 0-0 (.000).

NBA ALL-STAR RECORD

TEAM-YR	GP	MIN	FGM	FGA	PCT.	FTM	FTA	PCT.	OFF	DEF	REB	AST	PF-DQ	ST	BL	PTS	AVE
DET. '90	1	11	2	4	.500	0	0	0	3	1	4	1	1- 0	0	1	4	4

JOHN SALLEY

Position: Forward/Center
Height: 6'11"
Weight: 231
College: Georgia Tech '86 (Degree in Industrial Management)
High School: Canarsie HS, Brooklyn, NY
Birthdate: 05/16/64
Birthplace: Brooklyn, NY
When Drafted: First Round (11th Overall) Detroit, 1986
How Acquired: College Draft
Pro Experience: Four Years
Nickname: Spider
Marital Status: Single
Residence: Brooklyn, NY

LAST SEASON: Began the season as the team's starting power forward, only to be moved back to his familiar role off the bench... In the playoffs, he again had another outstanding post season... Started the first 12 games of the regular season, averaging 8.0 points and 6.2 rebounds per game... Then, finished the season by coming off the bench... For the third time in four seasons, he played in every game during the regular season... Scored better than double figures in 24 games... Has now blocked at least 100 shots in three of his first four seasons... Grabbed his career high of 13 rebounds on March 20...

AS A PRO: Started slowly in his rookie campaign, but has proved to be very consistent since that time... Has already recorded 487 blocked shots in his first three campaigns, which ranks him fourth on the all-time Pistons' blocked shots list... Had his best game as a pro during his rookie season when he scored 28 points, adding 10 rebounds and 5 blocked shots versus the Milwaukee Bucks on April 5, 1987... Set an all-time Pistons' playoff record with 10 offensive rebounds versus the Washington Bullets in the first round of the 1988 playoffs... In his four seasons, the Pistons have made four straight Eastern Conference Finals appearances and three straight Finals appearances...

AS A COLLEGIAN: Finished fourth on the all-time Georgia Tech scoring list with 1,587 points (12.7 points per game), third in all-time FG percentage (.587) and is the school's all-time shotblocker (243)... Started 27 games as a freshman and averaged 11.5 points and 5.7 rebounds per game... Had a career high of 28 points against Monmouth on 1-17-85... Set a school record in his junior season when he made .627 of his field goal attempts...

PERSONAL: One of the most outgoing and personable players on the Piston roster... Makes numerous personal appearances on behalf of the club throughout the year... Entered Georgia Tech as a 6-9, 185-pound forward and continued to add both size and strength... His nickname is Spider because of his long arms... Strengths are quickness, passing and shotblocking... Received his degree from Georgia Tech in the August of 1988... Runs a summer basketball camp... Aspiring comedian who makes appearances and comedy clubs during the year... His personal friends include Eddie Murphy and Spike Lee...

NBA CAREER RECORD

TEAM-YR	GP	MIN	FGM	FGA	PCT	FTM	FTA	PCT	OFF	DEF	REB	AVE	AST	PF-DQ	ST	BL	PTS	AVE	HI
DET.'87	82	1463	163	290	.562	105	171	.614	108	188	296	3.6	54	256- 5	44	125	431	5.3	28
DET.'88	82	2003	258	456	.566	185	261	.709	166	241	402	4.9	113	294- 4	53	137	701	8.5	19
DET.'89	67	1458	166	333	.498	135	195	.692	134	201	335	5	75	197- 3	40	72	467	7	19
DET.'90	82	1914	209	408	.512	174	244	.713	154	285	439	5.3	67	282- 7	51	153	593	7.2	21
TOTALS	313	6838	796	1487	.535	599	871	.688	562	915	1472	4.7	309	1029-19	188	487	2192	7	28

NBA HIGHS

		40	10	15		11	12		8	8	13		4		3	8	28		

3-POINT FIELD GOALS: 1986-87, 0-1 (.000); 1988-89, 0-2 (.000); 1989-90, 1-4 (.350). CAREER: 1-7 (.143); 1989, 0-2 (.000). CAREER: 0-3 (.000).0-2   (.000). CAREER: 0-3 (.000).0); 1989-90 , 1-4 (.350).CAREER: 1-7 (.143).

NBA PLAYOFF RECORD

TEAM-YR	GP	MINS	FGM	FGA	PCT	FTM	FTA	PCT	OFF	DEF	REB	AST	PF-DQ	ST	BL	PTS	AVE
DET.'87	15	311	33	66	.500	27	42	.643	30	42	72	11	60-1	3	17	93	6.2
DET.'88	23	623	56	104	.538	49	69	.710	64	91	155	21	88-2	15	37	161	7.0
DET.'89	17	392	58	99	.586	36	54	.667	34	45	79	9	56-0	9	25	152	8.9
DET.'90	20	547	58	122	.475	74	98	.755	57	60	117	20	76- 0	9	33	190	9.5
TOTALS	75	1873	205	391	.524	186	263	.707	185	238	423	61	282- 3	36	112	596	7.9

PLAYOFF HIGHS

		10	16		9	12				13	4				23	

3-POINT FIELD GOALS: 1987-88, 0-1 (.000); 1988-89, 0-0 (.000); 1989-90, 0-0 (.000).
CAREER: 0-1 (.000).

ISIAH THOMAS

Position: Guard
Height: 6'1"
Weight: 185
College: Indiana University '83 (Criminal Justice Degree)
High School: St. Joseph (Westchester, IL)
Birthdate: 4/30/61
Birthplace: Chicago, IL
When Drafted: First Round (2nd Overall) Detroit, 1981
How Acquired: College Draft
Pro Experience: Eight Years
Married: Lynn
Children: Joshua
Residence: Bloomfield Hills, MI

LAST SEASON: Captained the two-time World Champion Pistons... Most Valuable Player of the 1990 NBA Finals when he averaged 27.6 points, 7.0 assists and 5.2 assists against Portland... Tied an NBA Finals' record by connecting on four three-pointers during the third quarter of Game Four versus Portland... In the playoffs, he led the Pistons with 20.5 points per game average... Led the Pistons in scoring with 18.4 points per game and 9.4 assists in the regular season... During the last eight seasons, he's missed a total of 12 games despite various injuries... Connected on 42 of 136 three-pointers, both career highs... Appeared in his ninth straight NBA All-Star Game, scoring 15 points with 9 assists in the mid-season classic... Had 39 games of double figures in points and assists in the 1989-90 campaign...

AS A PRO: Needs just 1,134 points to become the leading scorer in Pistons' history... He will then surpass Bob Lanier's total of 15,488 points scored... Has been named to the NBA All-Star Team in each of his first nine seasons in the league... Two-time All-Star Game Most Valuable Player, winning the honor in 1984 and 1986... First was MVP in Denver in 1984 when he scored 21 points and added 15 assists... Then in 1986 in Dallas, he scored 30 points, adding 10 assists and 5 steals to gain the honor... All-time Pistons' leader in steals and assists, ranks third on the all-time Pistons' scoring list entering this season... Set an NBA record for assists in a single season (since broken by John Stockton) when he recorded 1,123 assists in 1984-85 for an average of 13.1 per game... Owns the Pistons' record for consecutive field goals made with 13... Holds the club record for points scored in a quarter with 24... Has had

some memorable playoff performances in leading the Pistons to five straight post-season appearances... Scored 25 points in the 3rd quarter of Game 6 versus the Lakers in the 1988 NBA Finals, setting a record for points in a quarter in a Finals game... Had 24 points in the 3rd quarter versus the Atlanta Hawks in the 1987 playoffs... In the 1990 NBA Finals, he scored 22 points in the third quarter... In Game One of the Finals he scored 16 points in the fourth quarter (finishing with 33) rallying Detroit from 10 points down with seven minutes remaining... But, maybe his most memorable playoff performance was in the 1984 playoffs versus the New York Knicks when he scored 16 points in 94 seconds in the fourth quarter of the decisive Game 5 of that series... Was drafted by the Pistons second overall in the 1981 NBA College Draft after leaving Indiana after his sophomore season... In his career with the Pistons, when he does not play, Detroit is 6-16...

AS A COLLEGIAN: Helped lead the Indiana Hoosiers to a 47-17 mark and an NCAA Championship (1981) with two Big Ten titles in his two seasons there... Missed only one game during his collegiate career and started all 63 games he played... All Big Ten as a sophomore... Was a consensus All-American after his sophomore season at Indiana... Top college scoring effort was 39 points versus the University of Michigan... Won 1981 NCAA Tournament Most Outstanding Player Award with 91 points in five games (18.2 points per game)... Member of the 1979 Pan-American Games Gold Medal Team, scoring 21 points in the title game, while leading the team in assists... Starter on the 1981 USA Olympic Team which had a 5-1 record against NBA All-Star Teams...

PERSONAL: His wife Lynn gave birth to the couple's first child (Joshua Isiah) during the 1988 NBA Finals... Prior to training camp in October of 1988 he signed a contract which will keep him in Detroit for the remainder of his basketball playing career... Youngest of nine children, one of the league's most vocal players in the fight against drug abuse, has made a 12-minute film entitled "Just Say No"... Married in July of 1985 to the former Lynn Kendall... Received his degree in Criminal Justice in August of 1987... Has numerous endorsements which include Toyota and Coca Cola... Isiah's Summer Classic All-Star Game in August of 1990 was played for the benefit of Comic Relief, benefitting the homeless... Authored the book "Bad Boys, An Inside Look at the Detroit Pistons 1988-89 Championship Season," co-authored by Pistons PR Director Matt Dobek...

NBA CAREER RECORD

TEAM-YR	GP	MIN	FGM	FGA	PCT	FTM	FTA	PCT	OFF	DEF	REB	AVE	AST	PF-DQ	ST	BLO	PTS	AVE	HI
DET.'82	72	2433	453	1068	.424	302	429	.704	57	152	209	2.9	565	253-2	150	17	1225	17.0	34
DET.'83	81	3093	725	1537	.472	368	518	.710	105	223	328	4.0	634	318-8	199	29	1854	22.9	46
DET.'84	82	3007	669	1448	.462	388	529	.733	103	224	327	4.0	914	324-8	204	33	1748	21.3	47
DET.'85	81	3089	646	1410	.458	399	493	.809	114	247	361	4.5	1123	288-8	187	25	1720	21.2	38
DET.'86	77	2790	609	1248	.488	365	462	.790	83	194	277	3.6	830	245-9	171	20	1609	20.9	39
DET.'87	81	3013	626	1353	.463	400	521	.768	82	237	319	3.9	813	251-5	153	20	1671	20.6	36
DET.'88	81	2927	621	1341	.463	305	394	.774	64	214	278	3.4	678	217-0	141	17	1577	19.5	42
DET.'89	80	2924	569	1227	.464	287	351	.818	49	224	273	3.4	663	209- 0	133	20	1458	18.2	37
DET.'90	81	2993	579	1322	.438	292	377	.774	74	234	308	3.8	765	206- 0	139	19	1492	18.4	37
TOTALS	716	26269	5497	11954	.459	3106	4074	.762	731	1949	2680	3.7	6985	2301-40	1477	200	14354	20	47

NBA HIGHS

		52	19	34		16	20		6	11	12		25		7	4	47		

3-POINT FIELD GOALS: 1981-82, 17-59 (.288); 1982-83, 36-125 (.288); 1983-84, 22-65 (.338); 1984-85, 29-113 (.257); 1986-87, 19-98 (.194); 1987-88, 30-97 (.309); 1988-89, 33-121 (.273); 1989-90, 42-136 (.309).
CAREER: 256-898 (.285)

NBA PLAYOFF RECORD

TEAM-YR	GP	MIN	FGM	FGA	PCT	FTM	FTA	PCT	OFF	DEF	REB	AST	PF-DQ	ST	BL	PTS	AVE
DET.'84	5	198	39	83	.470	27	35	.771	7	12	19	55	22-1	13	6	107	21.4
DET.'85	9	355	83	166	.500	47	62	.758	11	36	47	101	39-2	19	4	219	24.3
DET.'86	4	163	41	91	.451	24	36	.667	8	14	22	48	17-0	9	3	106	26.5
DET.'87	15	562	134	297	.451	83	110	.755	21	46	67	130	51-1	39	4	361	24.1
DET.'88	23	911	183	419	.437	125	151	.828	26	81	107	201	71-2	66	8	504	21.9
DET.'89	17	633	115	279	.412	71	96	.740	24	49	73	141	39-0	27	4	309	18.2
DET.'90	20	758	148	320	.463	81	102	.794	21	88	109	163	65- 1	43	7	409	20.5
TOTALS	93	3580	743	1655	.449	458	592	.773	118	326	444	839	304- 7	216	36	2015	21.6

PLAYOFF HIGHS

			18	33		13	17				12	16				43	

3-POINT FIELD GOALS: 1983-84, 2-6 (.333); 1984-85, 6-15 (.400); 1985-86, 0-5 (.000); 1986-87, 10-33 (.303); 1987-88, 13-44 (.295); 1988-89, 8-30 (.267); 1989-90, 32-68 (.471).
CAREER: 71-201 (.293) 31-103 (.301).

NBA ALL-STAR RECORD

TEAM-YR	GP	MIN	FGM	FGA	PCT	FTM	FTA	PCT	OFF	DEF	REB	AST	PF-DQ	ST	BL	PTS	AVE
DET.'82	1	17	5	7	.714	2	4	.500	1	0	1	4	1-0	3	0	12	12.0
DET.'83	1	29	9	14	.643	1	1	1.000	3	1	4	7	0-0	4	6	19	19.0
DET.'84	1	39	9	17	.529	3	3	1.000	2	3	5	15	4-0	4	0	21	21.0
DET.'85	1	25	9	14	.643	1	1	1.000	1	1	2	5	2-0	2	0	22	22.0
DET.'86	1	36	11	19	.579	8	9	.889	0	1	1	10	2-0	5	0	30	30.0
DET.'87	1	24	4	6	.667	8	9	.889	2	1	3	9	3-0	0	0	16	16.0
DET.'88	1	28	4	10	.400	0	0	.000	1	1	2	15	1-0	1	0	8	8.0
DET.'89	1	33	7	13	.538	4	6	.667	1	1	2	14	2-0	0	0	19	19.0
DET.'90	1	27	7	12	.583	0	0	.000	1	3	4	9	0-0	3	0	15	15
TOTALS	9	258	65	112	.580	27	33	.818	12	12	24	88	15-0	22	0	162	18

3-POINT FIELD GOALS: 1983-84, 0-2 (.000); 1984-85, 3-4 (.750); 1985-86, 0-1 (.000); 1988-89, 1-3 (.333); 1989-90, 1-1 (1.000).
CAREER: 5-11 (.455).

ANTHONY COOK

Position: Forward
Height: 6'9"
Weight: 190
College: University of Arizona '89
High School: Van Nuys, CA
Birthdate: 5/19/67
Birthplace: Los Angeles, CA
How Acquired: Trade for Kenny Battle and Michael Williams
Experience: Rookie
Marital Status: Single
Residence: Los Angeles, CA

LAST SEASON: Played in Greece during the 1989-90 season, after being unable to reach an agreement on a contract with the Pistons... The Pistons acquired his rights on draft day in 1989 from the Phoenix Suns in exchange for Michael Williams and the rights to Kenny Battle... Did not participate with the Pistons' entry in the California Summer Pro League... All-Pac 10 performer in both 1988 and 1989... Scored a career best 17.7 points in his final season at Arizona... Set school record with 80 blocked shots in his senior season... He played with the Pistons during the 1990 summer league hosted at The Palace...

AS A COLLEGIAN: The Pac 10's all-time career shot blocker... Led the Wildcats in rebounding during each of his final two campaigns... Scoring average improved steadily during each of his seasons at Arizona... Scored his career high of 31 points versus USC during his senior season... During his four-year career, he started 122 of 132 games...

PERSONAL: Sociology major... Product of Van Nuys High School in California... Hometown is Los Angeles...

COLLEGE CAREER RECORD

YEAR	GP	FGM	FGA	PCT	FTM	FTA	PCT	REB	AST	PTS	AVE
UofA '86	32	73	146	.500	48	73	.658	137	41	194	6.1
UofA '87	30	118	246	.480	54	100	.540	217	18	290	9.7
UofA '88	38	201	325	.618	126	176	.716	269	15	528	13.9
UofA '89	33	237	377	.629	104	166	.627	238	12	578	17.5
TOTALS	133	629	1094	.576	332	515	.645	861	86	1590	12.0

MARK HUGHES

Position: Center/Forward
Height: 6'8"
Weight: 235
College: University of Michigan '89
High School: Reeths Puffer High School (Muskegon, MI)
Birthdate: 10/5/66
Birthplace: Muskegon, MI
How Acquired: Free Agent
Experience: Rookie
Marital Status: Single
Residence: Muskegon, MI

LAST SEASON: Was the final player cut from the Pistons during training camp in 1989... Will again make a serious bid for the 12-man roster... In 1989-90 he then played in Europe after being released by the Pistons... Co-captained the 1989 NCAA Champion Michigan Wolverines... Averaged 6.8 points and 4.1 rebounds for the Wolverines during his senior season... Signed as a free agent in July of 1989 then again signed during the summer of 1990... After not being selected in the June draft, he was invited to participate in the Pistons' free agent camp in July... After impressing the coaching staff in the California Summer Pro League in 1989, he was signed to a contract and invited to veteran's camp in October before being released...

AS A COLLEGIAN: Four-year performer at the University of Michigan... After starting 47 games in his sophomore and junior seasons, he started just four contests in his final campaign... Scored his career high of 17 points versus Purdue in his senior season... Missed the second half of his freshman season due to arthroscopic knee surgery...

PERSONAL: High school product of Muskegon Reeths Puffer... Led Reeths Puffer to semi-finals of the state tournament in his senior season... Sociology major at Michigan...

COLLEGE CAREER RECORD

YEAR	GP	FGM	FGA	PCT	FTM	FTA	PCT	REB	AST	PTS	AVE
UofM '86	14	12	24	.500	7	9	.778	18	2	31	2.2
UofM '87	32	86	158	.544	22	29	.759	192	42	194	6.1
UofM '88	34	65	123	.526	26	43	.605	133	33	156	4.6
TOTALS	80	163	305	.534	55	81	.679	343	77	381	4.8

LANCE BLANKS

Position: Guard
Height: 6'4"
Weight: 195
College: Texas '90
High School: McCullough HS, The Woodlands, TX
Birthdate: 09/09/66
Birthplace: Houston, TX
When Drafted: First Round (26th Overall), Detroit, 1990
Hou Acquired: College Draft
Pro Experience: Rookie
Marital Status: Single
Residence: Houston, TX

LAST SEASON: Selected by the Pistons (26th overall) in the first round of the 1990 NBA Draft... Will vie for the fourth guard spot on the Pistons' roster... Averaged 20.3 points, 4.3 rebounds and 3.0 assists as a senior to help lead the Longhorns to the Midwest regional finals in the NCAA Tournament... Finished eighth on the all-time University of Texas scoring list with 1,322 points... His 20.0 scoring average was the third highest in school history...

AS A COLLEGIAN: Sat out the 1987-88 season after transferring from Virginia where he saw limited action during his two seasons with the Cavaliers... Finished as the second leading scorer in the Southwest Conference behind teammate Travis Mays as a junior... In that 1988-89 season, he recorded 111 steals, two shy of the conference record set by Clyde Drexler... Scored 30 or more points in nine games during his collegiate career...

PERSONAL: His father Sid, a former NFL player, represents his son in contract negotiations...

COLLEGE CAREER RECORD

YEAR	GP	FGM	FGA	PCT	FTM	FTA	PCT	REB	AST	PTS	AVE
VA '86	14	14	32	.438	6	12	.500	15	6	34	2.4
VA '87	24	13	25	.520	2	7	.286	18	14	28	1.2
TX '89	34	237	527	.450	119	174	.684	191	145	671	19.7
TX '90	32	206	512	.402	161	202	.797	136	96	651	20.3
TOTALS	104	470	1096	.429	288	395	.729	360	261	1384	13.3

NOTE: SAT OUT 1987-88 SEASON AFTER TRANSFERRING FROM VIRGINIA, WHERE HE SAW LIMITED ACTION FOR TWO YEARS.

PISTONS ALL-TIME RECORDS AGAINST NBA OPPONENTS 1957-1989

TEAM	79-80	80-81	81-82	82-83	83-84	84-85	85-86	86-87	87-88	88-89	89-90	TOTAL	HOME	ROAD	NEUTRAL
ATL*	0-6	2-4	4-2	3-3	4-2	5-1	2-4	3-3	4-2	5-1	2-3	104-133	55-51	38-68	11-14
BOS	0-6	1-4	0-6	3-3	3-3	2-4	1-4	2-3	3-3	3-1	2-2	53-155	31-66	17-64	5-25
CHA	—	—	—	—	—	—	—	—	—	4-0	2-0	6-0	3-0	3-0	—
CHI	1-1	1-5	6-0	4-2	5-1	3-3	4-2	3-3	4-2	6-0	4-1	81-62	50-19	29-41	2-2
CLE	0-6	3-3	5-1	5-1	5-1	5-1	5-1	5-1	5-1	3-3	4-1	66-34	37-15	29-19	—
DAL	—	2-0	1-1	0-2	2-0	2-0	2-0	1-1	1-1	2-0	1-1	14-6	8-2	6-4	—
DEN	1-1	0-2	1-1	0-2	1-1	2-0	1-1	2-0	1-1	1-1	2-0	17-17	10-7	7-10	—
GS#	1-1	0-2	2-0	2-0	1-1	2-0	1-1	1-1	2-0	1-1	1-1	78-104	48-32	23-52	7-20
HOU	1-5	1-1	2-0	2-0	1-1	1-1	1-1	1-1	1-1	1-1	1-1	46-39	30-10	12-28	4-1
IND	1-5	2-4	2-4	4-2	4-2	6-0	5-1	3-3	3-3	4-2	4-1	43-34	30-9	13-25	—
LAC!	0-2	1-1	2-0	1-1	2-0	1-1	2-0	2-0	1-1	2-0	1-1	41-21	24-7	17-14	—
LAL%	0-2	0-2	0-2	0-2	1-1	1-1	1-1	1-1	0-2	2-0	1-1	73-126	32-53	26-61	15-12
MIA	—	—	—	—	—	—	—	—	—	2-0	3-1	5-1	3-0	2-1	—
MIL	1-1	1-5	2-4	3-3	3-2	3-3	2-4	3-3	4-2	2-4	3-2	50-76	34-29	16-45	0-2
MIN	—	—	—	—	—	—	—	—	—	2-0	2-0	2-0	1-0	1-0	—
NJ	2-4	3-3	2-4	3-2	1-4	1-5	4-2	5-1	5-1	4-0	4-0	40-32	22-14	18-18	—
NY	2-4	1-5	3-3	1-5	4-2	3-2	4-1	6-0	4-2	0-4	4-0	96-116	52-44	32-59	12-12
ORL	—	—	—	—	—	—	—	—	—	5-0	5-0	5-0	3-0	2-0	—
PHIL+	1-5	1-4	2-3	0-6	3-3	1-5	2-4	5-0	4-1	5-0	1-3	77-133	46-45	18-68	13-20
PHOE	0-2	0-2	0-2	1-1	2-0	2-0	0-2	1-1	2-0	2-0	2-0	40-39	24-16	15-23	1-0
PORT	0-2	0-2	0-2	1-1	1-1	1-1	1-1	0-2	1-1	1-1	1-1	32-31	22-10	10-21	—
SAC$	0-2	2-1	2-0	0-2	1-1	1-1	0-2	1-1	2-0	2-0	2-0	104-96	61-21	27-51	16-24
SA	2-4	0-2	0-2	1-1	1-1	1-1	1-1	1-1	1-1	1-1	2-0	14-22	7-11	7-11	—
SEA	0-2	0-2	1-1	0-2	1-1	1-1	2-0	2-0	1-1	2-0	1-1	41-40	25-14	11-26	5-0
UTAH@	1-1	0-2	1-1	0-2	1-1	0-2	1-1	1-1	2-0	2-0	1-1	23-19	15-6	8-13	—
WASH=	2-4	1-5	2-0	3-2	3-3	3-3	4-2	3-2	3-2	5-0	4-0	87-92	48-29	25-54	14-9
TOTALS	16-66	21-61	39-43	37-45	49-33	46-36	46-36	52-30	54-28	63-19	59-23	1238-1427	721-510	412-776	105-141

*ST.LOUIS 1957-68 #PHILADELPHIA 1957-62, SAN FRANCISCO 1962-79 $CINCINNATI 1957-72, KANSAS CITY 1972-85 %MINNEAPOLIS 1957-60 +SYRACUSE 1957-63 BUFFALO 1970-78, SANDIEGO 1979-84 @NEW ORLEANS 1974-79 =CHICAGO 1961-63, BALTIMORE 1963-74 #PHILADELPHIA 1957-62, SAN FRANCISCO 1962-79.

WILLIAM DAVIDSON

MANAGING PARTNER

After 15 long years, Pistons Managing Partner William Davidson achieved his ultimate goal: A 1989 World Championship for his Detroit Pistons. One year later, he became the owner of only the third team in history to repeat as NBA Champions.

Detroit's 1989 and 1990 World Championships can be directly attributed to Davidson, the club's majority owner since 1974. Under Davidson's direction, the Pistons have been considered one of the league's elite franchises for the last four years.

Now, after Detroit won its first-ever NBA Championship, never in the history of the franchise has the future looked brighter. In 1988-89, the Pistons began play in The Palace of Auburn Hills, a state-of-the-art arena built with Davidson's financial support. The Pistons are coming off the three most successful seasons in the history of the franchise.

For the second straight season, the Pistons advanced to The NBA Finals, and after finishing second in 1988, Davidson's accomplished the ultimate in 1989, a first-ever NBA Championship. The Pistons have now won the Central Division in each of the last two seasons, including a club record 63-19 record in 1988-89. Including the playoffs, the Pistons were 78-21 for the year, recording one of the single most successful seasons in the history of the NBA.

Davidson acquired the Detroit Pistons in 1974 from the late Fred Zollner, the man who founded the team in Fort Wayne in the 1940s and moved the franchise to Detroit in 1957-58.

Interested in a wide variety of sports, Davidson is one of the most knowledgeable heads of an NBA franchise. He has studied the talents and abilities of players and coaches in the league and has some very astute observations.

The Pistons' majority owner likes success and has known it in his business interests. That's why now, the success of the Detroit Pistons comes as no surprise to those who are aware of Davidson's ability to manage people.

Educated in Business and Law, Davidson received a Bachelor's Degree in Business Administration from the University of Michigan and earned a Juris Doctor's Degree from Wayne State University.

After three years, Davidson gave up his law practice to take over a wholesale drug company; he rescued it from bankruptcy and turned it around in three years. Then, he took over a surgical supply company which was on the verge of bankruptcy and saved it as well. The next step was to take the Guardian Glass Company, the family business, turning it around in two years by paying off all debts and heading it on a profitable growth path which the company enjoys now. Even today, Guardian Industries

remains the flagship of his business interests.

Davidson expects his previous track record to help pave the way for the Pistons and The Palace. The success he has enjoyed has come from a proven talent for hiring competent managers and placing the responsibility with them. That is the same formula he has used with the Detroit Pistons for the past 14 years and now expects to do the same with an arena he believes will be one of the best in the world.

The athletic interests of Davidson date back many years and have continued alongside his business career. He was a high school and college track man and played freshman football in the Navy during World War II. Davidson was an initial inductee into the Jewish Sports Hall of Fame.

Davidson's management talents are continually on display in NBA circles, where he is active on the player relations and finance committees. He was a member of the committee which selected former NBA Commissioner Lawrence O'Brien in 1975. Davidson, who can usually be found sitting courtside at most Pistons' home games, is active in numerous community and charitable affairs.

The Detroit Pistons ownership group includes Legal Counsel Oscar Feldman, and Advisory Board Members Warren Coville, Ted Ewald, Milt Dresner, Bud Gerson, Dorothy Gerson, David Mondry, Eugene Mondry, Ann Newman, Herb Tyner and William Wetsman.

JACK McCLOSKEY
GENERAL MANAGER

Defense is one trademark of the two-time World Champion Detroit Pistons. Depth and bench strength are the others. If the defensive mind-set is credited to the coaching staff, the depth and bench strength have to be credited to general manager Jack McCloskey. Entering his 12th season as the Pistons' General Manager, McCloskey has built the club into one of the elite franchises in the NBA.

Throughout the NBA, McCloskey has acquired the nickname "Trader Jack" because of his ability to swing a deal and then have the acquired player make an immediate impact upon the Pistons' team. In 1988-89, his acquiring of Mark Aguirre in mid-season only added to his reputation. After the trade, the Pistons finished with a 45-8 record on their way to a first-ever NBA Championship.

When the Pistons needed an astute basketball mind to direct the on-court fortunes of the club, Managing Partner William Davidson appointed NBA veteran McCloskey as General Manager on December 11, 1979. Over those past 10 years, McCloskey's trades have often been the talk of the league due to the success of the Pistons on the court.

At the time of the announcement of McCloskey as the team's General Manager, Davidson called the addition "a positive step in the building of our franchise to an NBA Championship level." After 10 hard years of work, McCloskey assembled the 1989 World Champions. Additionally, the Pistons are two-time Eastern Conference Champions and two-time Central Division Champions. Indeed, the Pistons have arrived as a Championship level basketball team.

In each of the last three seasons, McCloskey has been considered among the top executives in the NBA. With his ability to select top-notch collegiate talent through the NBA draft, McCloskey has been able to keep the Pistons at a championship level. In 1981-82, he was recognized by his peers as one of the league's top general managers when he was voted runnerup in the Sporting News' Executive of the Year balloting. In each succeeding season, McCloskey has been considered for the award.

McCloskey's duties include authority over all basketball-playing aspects of the Pistons organization including coaching, player personnel, all scouting and trades.

A native of Mahanoy City, PA, McCloskey came to the Pistons from the Indiana Pacers where he served as an assistant to head coach Bob Leonard during the 1979-80 season. Previously, he assisted Jerry West, now the general manager of the Los Angeles Lakers, for three seasons.

Upon joining the Pistons, McCloskey, a 1948 graduate of the University of Pennsylvania, had 23 years of coaching experience behind him. During his playing days, he was an acknowledged all-around athlete, playing basketball and football at Penn, plus eight years in the American and Eastern Basketball League. His career as a player also includes a brief stint in the NBA and four years

of professional basketball in the Philadelphia A's organization. McCloskey and diminutive guard Charlie Criss rank as the Eastern League's only two-time MVP's. His Eastern League teammates included current Pistons' Director of Scouting Stan Novak and former Indiana Pacers' Head Coach Jack Ramsay.

It was after a highly successful high school coaching career that McCloskey returned to Penn in 1956, inheriting a team that went from 7-19, then 13-12 and 12-14 before seven straight winning seasons with Ivy League first-division finishes annually. In his final season, McCloskey led the 1965-66 Penn team to a 19-6 campaign, the most wins since 1954-55, capturing the Ivy League title. His teams were 87-53 in Ivy League play and won the Philadelphia Big Five Title in 1963 on their way to an overall 146-105 record in 10 seasons.

McCloskey's next stop was Wake Forest, where he transformed the lowly Deacons into an Atlantic Coast Conference contender. After a 14-39 mark in his first two years, he followed with four successful seasons in the rugged ACC while compiling a 56-50 slate. His assistants were Billy Packer and the late Neil Johnston, former NBA scoring ace of the old Warriors.

His next chore was to take over the expansion Portland Trail Blazers in 1972-73 for two painful building seasons. The Pacific Division team was an eventual NBA champion. In his tenure with the Lakers, he served as the offensive coordinator for two seasons and defensive coordinator for a year as the Lakers bounced back from two losing seasons with three winning campaigns.

Jack and wife Leslie make their home in West Bloomfield. One of the top senior tennis players in the state, Jack was a 1981 inductee into the Jerry Wolman Chapter of the Pennsylvania Sports Hall of Fame.

THOMAS S. WILSON
CHIEF EXECUTIVE OFFICER

Over the last seven seasons, the Detroit Pistons have been one of the most successfully marketed franchises in the National Basketball Association. Not only has that been proven through five league-leading attendance marks and sellouts every night, but also by the current all-time high interest mark in the club. One of the major factors behind the financial success the Detroit Pistons now enjoy is Chief Executive Officer Thomas S. Wilson.

In 1989-90, as Detroit repeated as World Champions, the club had another back-to-back record: again selling out every home game during the regular season and playoffs. The Pistons have now sold out The Palace 102 straight games.

Over the last 10 years with the Pistons, Wilson's duties and responsibilities have continued to increase dramatically. As the Pistons' chief executive officer, Wilson oversees all the administrative, marketing, broadcasting and promotional efforts of the organization.

Wilson's workload increased dramatically with the opening of The Palace of Auburn Hills in 1988. New home of the Detroit Pistons, the Palace was designed largely around Wilson's input. The Pistons have been able to customize the new facility to provide the finest sightlines and comfort levels for basketball of any arena in the country. Wilson took on the responsibility of staffing the arena and of developing the philosophies that will present all of the arena's events in the finest manner possible. Now, the state-of-the-art Palace has been cited as one of the best arenas in the world.

Wilson spent much of the previous three years traveling around the United States and Canada studying all aspects of various arenas and incorporating the best features of each into the Pistons' new home.

"The success of the Detroit Pistons has been very rewarding to the organization, to me personally, but the challenge of designing the finest facility ever built for basketball and other events has been the most exciting project I have been involved with.

"We began with the Pistons in the final season at Cobo, lived through the down season and shared the success of the current era, which culminated with a World Championship in 1989. I know our staff anxiously awaits the opportunity as we move into the brightest time in our history."

Wilson joined the Pistons in 1978 and watched the team linger through several poor seasons. After a 16-66 season, the Pistons' attendance figures dropped below 6,000 per game. But, when the team drafted Isiah Thomas in 1981 and made several other key acquisitions through trades and subsequent drafts, the future began to look much brighter.

Under Wilson's leadership, the Pistons have now led the NBA in attendance in each of the last five seasons.

The Pistons set the all-time NBA record for attendance in 1987-88 becoming the first NBA franchise to attract one million fans during the regular season. By averaging 26,012 fans per game, the Pistons have established an NBA record that may never be broken.

The Pistons' outstanding success in broadcasting is also headed by Wilson. When the Pistons moved both the television and radio broadcast in-house he was responsible for overseeing all aspects. Over the last two seasons, the Pistons have set franchise records in television ratings.

He continues to be involved with broadcasting as he serves as the color commentator for all Pistons' games on Pro-Am Sports Systems (PASS). In 1989-90, Wilson will team up with Channel 4's Fred McLeod to telecast the games on cable.

A native Detroiter, Wilson received his bachelor's of business administration from Wayne State University. Prior to joining the Pistons, he worked for both the Los Angeles Lakers and the Los Angeles Kings, and the Forum. He also worked in films and television in California, appearing in over 40 television programs.

An inveterate runner, he has participated in two Detroit Free Press Marathons. Tom and his wife Linda reside in Rochester Hills with daughters Kasey and Brooke.

CHUCK DALY

HEAD COACH

In 1990, Chuck Daly took his place in history by becoming only the third coach in the NBA to win back-to-back championships. Over seven seasons with the Pistons, he has become the most successful coach in the team's 31-year history.

Before he came to Detroit in 1983, the Pistons had never recorded back-to-back winning seasons. All that changed in Daly's seven years, as the Pistons have not had a losing season since and have made the playoffs in each season of his tenure.

Daly made another strong bid for Coach-of-the-Year honors by following up 1988-89's club record 63-19, with a 59-23 mark, tied for second best in the league in 1989-90. In the playoffs, the Pistons went 15-5 on their way to repeating. With the retirement of Pat Riley at the end of 1990, Daly became the winningest active coach in the playoffs, 62-31 (.667).

In 1990, the Pistons set the top two winning streaks in franchise history. During the months of January, February and March the Pistons won 13 games and then 12 in a row with only one loss in between. The 25-1 streak was the third best in the history of the NBA and lasted from January 23 through March 21.

The Pistons have now enjoyed the four best seasons in the club's history under Daly's direction (1987 and '88,'89,'90). The Pistons are the three-time defending Eastern Conference champs and also the three-time defending Central Division champs. Prior to that, the Pistons had never won a division title.

After tying the club record with 52 wins in 1986-87, the Pistons recorded a 54-28 mark in 1987-88. In 1988-89, the Pistons became one of the few teams in the league to record a 60-win season, as Detroit went 63-19 in the regular season. The Pistons were 15-2 in the playoffs on their way to their first NBA title. His seven-year regular season coaching record stands at 369-215.

Daly was named the head coach of the Pistons on May 17, 1983, replacing Scotty Robertson. In his first season with the club in 1983-84, Daly improved their record by 12 games, as the Pistons finished with a 49-33 mark and a post-season appearance. Then in the next two campaigns, the team finished with 46-36 records and post-season appearances. The Pistons went on to enjoy the most successful seasons in the history of the franchise in Daly's fourth, fifth, sixth and seventh seasons.

He brought much experience to Detroit. Prior to joining the Pistons, Daly spent four-plus seasons as an assistant to Billy Cunningham and the Philadelphia 76ers. The Sixers were 236-104 in regular-season play during those four-plus years, winning two division titles and finishing second twice. The Sixers also logged a 32-21 playoff record in the four seasons before he departed for the Cleveland Cavaliers' head coaching job. Daly was regarded by the Sixers as especially adept at setting up offenses and defenses for particular opponents.

In Daly's six seasons (1971-77) as the head coach of the University of Pennsylvania, his teams won

four Ivy League titles and were runners-up twice. Penn won three Big Five Championships outright and tied for another under Daly's supervision, while compiling an overall record of 125-38 (.744 percentage) and won 20 of 25 Big Five Titles (.800 percentage). In his first season as the Penn head coach, he led the Quakers to a 25-3 record, a No. 3 ranking nationally and first place in the Eastern Collegiate Athletic Conference (ECAC). Daly led Penn to more NCAA berths and Big Five titles than any other head coach at Penn.

Daly was the head coach at Boston College for two seasons (1969-71) with a 26-26 record. He had served as an assistant at Duke for seven years (1963-69), first as freshman coach, then four years as the varsity assistant coach.

Daly graduated from Bloomsburg University after starting his collegiate career at St. Bonaventure; he earned a master's degree at Penn State and began his coaching career at Punxsutawney (Pennsylvania) High School.

Daly, a native of Kane, Pennsylvania, has become a very popular speaker on the banquet circuit and has numerous endorsements with sponsors.

Chuck, and his wife Terry, reside in West Bloomfield. They have one daughter, Cydney, a Penn State graduate who works for Revlon.

WILL ROBINSON

ADMINISTRATIVE ASSISTANT TO THE GENERAL MANAGER

Will Robinson has dedicated his life to basketball. Recently, the game has been returning the favor as the Robinson legacy continues.

In the spring of 1982, Will was inducted into the Michigan Sports Hall of Fame, the supreme honor in the state where he enjoyed most of his coaching success. That success has continued during his years with the Pistons where he currently is the team's director of community relations and the administrative assistant to General Manager Jack McCloskey. His duties include scouting, special assignments and working the Pistons' training camp.

The list of names of the athletes who played for Robinson reads like a Who's Who in sports. His teams were usually tagged with the title "Champion."

Robinson's Detroit Miller High School team, paced by the great Sammy Gee, won the city championship over St. Joseph's High School in 1947, drawing 16,249 to Olympia Stadium. The game turnout set a Michigan attendance mark that stood until the Pistons moved to the Pontiac Silverdome in 1978.

When Robinson moved to Detroit Pershing High School, the name changed but the results were the same as his teams continued rolling up championships, winning at an 85 percent clip.

In 1963, Pershing and the PSL returned to state tournament play, and the team went to the final four of the state tournament led by Mel Daniels (former ABA center), Ted Sizemore (major league baseball player) and Willie Iverson (ABL Miami Floridians.)

One of the strongest high school basketball teams ever asembled played for Robinson in 1967. The five all later played in professional sports. Spencer Haywood and Ralph Simpson (both NBA and ABA), Glen Doughty and Paul Seals (pro football) and Marvin Lane (major league baseball) won the state championship.

The Robinson name soon was recognized nationally, and Illinois State Athletic Director Milt Weisbecker gave the coach a chance at the big-time collegiate game. Robinson became the first black coach to direct a major college team and recorded five consecutive winning seasons. Among his standouts were All-Pro guard Doug Collins, one of the many Olympians Robinson produced, and Bubbles Hawkins, who later played guard with the New Jersey Nets.

There have been other standouts: Wayne State all-time great Charlie Primas, Baltimore Colt All-Pro Big Daddy Lipscomb, Wayne State VP Noah Brown, Olympians Lorenzo Wright and Charley Fonville and political advisor Ofield Dukes. The athletic field was not the only place where Robinson was developing outstanding individuals. He is just as proud of the 25 Detroit police officers who

played for him, the college grads with Ph.D.s attached to their names and the sons of his players who are now headline-makers.

Robinson's induction into the Michigan Sports Hall of Fame marked the fifth such honor for him. He was previously tapped for the Michigan High School Coaches' Hall of Fame, the West Virginia State Hall of Fame, the Illinois State Hall of Fame and the Dapper Dan Hall of Fame.

Robinson, who makes his home in Detroit, has one son, William Jr., the coordinator of academic programs at the University of Michigan.

Robinson's induction into the Michigan Sports Hall of Fame marked the seventh such honor bestowed him. The others include: The Michigan High School Coaches Hall of Fame. The West Virginia State Hall of Fame, The Illinois State Hall of Fame, The Upper Ohio Valley Dapper Dan Hall of Fame, The Afro-American Sports Hall of Fame and the Michigan High School Basketball Hall of Fame.

BRENDAN SUHR

ASSISTANT COACH

Beginning his second season as top assistant for the back-to-back World Champions is eleven year NBA veteran Brendan Suhr.

Suhr joined the Pistons in January of the 1988-89 season when then top assistant Dick Versace left to take over the head coaching duties for the Indiana Pacers.

Suhr is considered one of the top technicians in the game and specializes in designing offenses and defenses that will neutralize Pistons opponents. He is one of the best teachers in the league and will be on the bench for every game with duties that include practice and game coaching as well as advance scouting. He also runs the Pistons rookie/free agent camps during the summer and has a big role in developing young talent.

Before joining Chuck Daly's staff, Suhr served as Assistant General Manager and Director of Scouting for the Atlanta Hawks. He joined the Hawks in the 1979-80 season as an assistant coach and held that position for nine consecutive NBA seasons before being appointed Asst. General Manager in July of 1988.

In college, Suhr was a standout guard and led his Montclair State team to two NCAA Tournament berths. As a senior, he was named team captain and most valuable player. Also as a senior, he led his team in assists and was second in the nation in free throw percentage.

After graduation, Brendan spent one season as an assistant at the University of Detroit before moving to Fairfield

University (CT). At Fairfield he earned his Masters Degree in Educational Administration in 1979. Six years of college coaching saw his teams compile a 106-57 cumulative record and a berth in the 1978 NIT Tournament for Fairfield.

Suhr and his wife, Brenda, have two children, Christina and Brendan Kelly (B.K.) and make their home in the Rochester area. Brendan is one of the NBA's most dedicated distance runners and spends much of his time in the off season with basketball camps and clinics.

BRENDAN MALONE

ASSISTANT COACH

Brendan Malone, a 20-year coaching veteran, begins his third season as an assistant to Chuck Daly.

Malone, one of the most well-liked men in the NBA, replaced Ron Rothstein in 1988 when Rothstein took over head coaching responsibilities for the Miami Heat. Malone's duties for the back-to-back World Champions will include advance scouting of all Pistons' opponents, game and practice responsibilities and player development.

He is considered an excellent basketball man and very knowledgeable concerning the technical aspects of the NBA. Malone is an outstanding teacher and is entrusted with job of advising players on shooting, rebounding and developing their skills.

For the past two seasons, Malone was an assistant coach and scout for the New York Knicks. His duties with the Knicks included scouting college talent and advance scouting NBA opponents in addition to his bench coaching duties.

Malone joined the Knickerbockers in 1986, following a two-year stint as the head coach at the University of Rhode Island.

Prior to coaching at Rhode Island, Brendan was an assistant coach under Jim Boeheim at Syracuse University for six seasons. From 1978 through 1984, the Orangemen posted a record of 134-52 (72 percent), including three NCAA Tournament appearances. Malone was an assistant coach at Fordham University in 1976-77 and at Yale University in 1977-78.

He began his coaching career at Power Memorial Academy in New York City, where he remained for 10 successful seasons.

In Malone's final six seasons at Power Memorial, his teams won a pair of city championships, and he was a three-time New York City "Coach of the Year."

Malone played high school basketball at Rice High School in New York City, and earned his Bachelor's Degree at Iona College in New Rochelle. He earned his master's degree in physical education at New York University. Brendan and his wife Maureen have six children and plan to make their home in metro Detroit.

1990-91 Schedule

NOV.	2	MILWAUKEE (Fri., 8:00)
	3	CLEVELAND (Sat., 7:30)
	7	@ Seattle (Tue., 10:00)
	*9	@ L.A. Clippers (Wed., 10:30)
	13	MIAMI (Tue., 7:30)
	16	@ New Jersey (Fri., 7:30)
	17	ATLANTA (Sat., 7:30)
	20	@ MIAMI (Tue., 7:30)
	21	@ Indiana (Wed., 7:30)
	23	WASHINGTON (Fri., 8:00)
	25	SACRAMENTO (Sun., 7:30)
	27	@ Atlanta (Tue., 7:30)
	28	NEW YORK (Wed., 7:30)
	*30	PHILADELPHIA (Fri., 8:00)
DEC.	1	@ Washington (Sat., 7:30)
	*4	@ L.A. Lakers (Tue., 10:30)
	5	@ Utah (Wed., 9:30)
	7	@ Golden State (Fri., 10:30)
	8	@ Scramento (Sat., 10:30)
	11	SAN ANTONIO (Tue., 7:30)
	*14	@ Boston (Fri., 8:00)
	18	@ Milwaukee (Tue., 8:30)
	19	CHICAGO (Wed., 7:30)
	21	ATLANTA (Fri., 8:00)
	22	@ Philadelphia (Sat., 7:30)
	#25	@ Chicago (Tue., 3:30)
	26	CHARLOTTE (Wed., 7:30)
	28	@ Minnesota (Fri., 8:00)
	29	HOUSTON (Sat., 7:30)
JAN.	2	DENVER (Wed., 7:30)
	4	@ Cleveland (Fri., 7:30)
	5	NEW JERSEY (Sat., 7:30)
	*8	@ Charlotte (Tue., 8:00)
	*11	PORTLAND (Fri., 8:00)
	12	MIAMI (Sat., 7:30)
	14	@ Dallas (Mon. 8:30)
	17	@ Houston (Thu., 8:30)
	18	@ Phoenix (Fri, 9:30)
	21	BOSTON (Mon., 7:30)
	*23	@ Boston (Wed., 8:00)
	25	DALLAS (Fri., 8:00)
	26	@ Orlando (Sat., 7:30)
	28	WASHINGTON (Mon., 7:30)
	30	CLEVELAND (Wed., 7:30)

FEB.	*1	@ Washington (Fri, 8:00)
	#3	PHOENIX (Sun., 1:00)
	5	PHILADELPHIA (Tue., 7:30)
	*7	CHICAGO (Thu., 8:00)
	13	INDIANA (Wed., 7:30)
	14	@ Milwaukee (Thu., 8:30)
	#17	@ New York (Sun., 1:30)
	18	SEATTLE (Mon., 7:30)
	20	ATLANTA (Wed., 7:30)
	22	@ Charlotte (Fri., 7:30)
	#24	L.A. LAKERS (Sun., 3:30)
	26	@ Cleveland (Tue., 7:30)
	28	@ Miami (Thu., 7:30)
MAR.	1	UTAH (Fri., 8:00)
	3	L.A. CLIPPERS (Sun., 7:00)
	6	NEW YORK (Wed., 7:30)
	9	@ Indiana (Sat., 7:30)
	11	MILWAUKEE (Mon., 7:30)
	13	CHARLOTTE (Wed., 7:30)
	14	@ New Jersey (Thu., 7:30)
	16	ORLANDO (Sat., 7:30)
	*20	@ Philadelphia (Wed., 8:00)
	22	NEW JERSEY (Fri., 8:00)
	#24	@ San Antonio (Sun., 1:00)
	25	@ Denver (Mon., 9:30)
	27	INDIANA (Wed., 7:30)
	29	GOLDEN STATE (Fri., 8:00)
APR.	2	@ Charlotte (Tue., 7:30)
	5	MINNESOTA (Fri., 8:00)
	6	@ New York (Sat., 8:30)
	9	@ Milwaukee (Tue., 8:30)
	10	CLEVELAND (Wed., 7:30)
	12	CHICAGO (Fri., 8:00)
	#14	@ Indiana (Sun., 3:30)
	16	BOSTON (Tue., 7:30)
	19	@ Atlanta (Fri., 8:00)
	#21	@ Chicago (Sun., 3:30)

All Times are Detroit Times.   Home games in caps.

*TNT Games   #NBC Games